Clyde Weber Votaw

The Primitive Era of Christianity

As Recorded in the Acts of the Apostles, 30-63 A.D.

Clyde Weber Votaw

The Primitive Era of Christianity
As Recorded in the Acts of the Apostles, 30-63 A.D.

ISBN/EAN: 9783337099718

Printed in Europe, USA, Canada, Australia, Japan

Cover: Foto ©Lupo / pixelio.de

More available books at **www.hansebooks.com**

THE
PRIMITIVE ERA OF CHRISTIANITY

AS RECORDED IN THE ACTS OF THE
APOSTLES 30–63 A. D.

A SERIES OF INDUCTIVE STUDIES IN THE ENGLISH BIBLE

BY

CLYDE W. VOTAW, Ph.D.

INSTRUCTOR IN NEW TESTAMENT LITERATURE IN THE
UNIVERSITY OF CHICAGO

CHICAGO
The University of Chicago Press
1898

INDUCTIVE STUDIES IN THE ACTS

CHRONOLOGY OF THE CHRISTIAN CHURCH, 30-100 A. D.

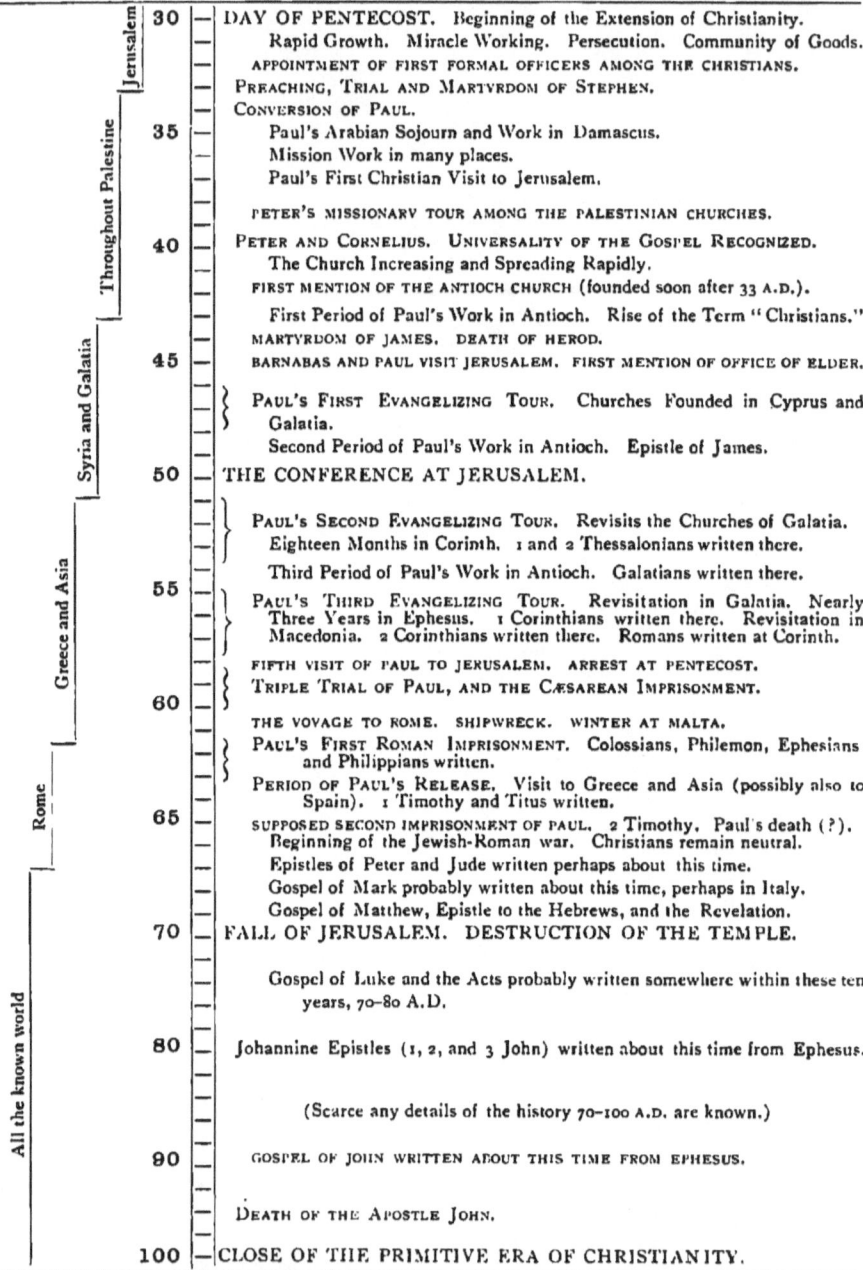

Jerusalem	30	DAY OF PENTECOST. Beginning of the Extension of Christianity. Rapid Growth. Miracle Working. Persecution. Community of Goods.
		APPOINTMENT OF FIRST FORMAL OFFICERS AMONG THE CHRISTIANS.
		PREACHING, TRIAL AND MARTYRDOM OF STEPHEN.
		CONVERSION OF PAUL.
	35	Paul's Arabian Sojourn and Work in Damascus.
		Mission Work in many places.
		Paul's First Christian Visit to Jerusalem.
		PETER'S MISSIONARY TOUR AMONG THE PALESTINIAN CHURCHES.
	40	PETER AND CORNELIUS. UNIVERSALITY OF THE GOSPEL RECOGNIZED. The Church Increasing and Spreading Rapidly.
		FIRST MENTION OF THE ANTIOCH CHURCH (founded soon after 33 A.D.).
		First Period of Paul's Work in Antioch. Rise of the Term "Christians."
		MARTYRDOM OF JAMES. DEATH OF HEROD.
	45	BARNABAS AND PAUL VISIT JERUSALEM. FIRST MENTION OF OFFICE OF ELDER.
		PAUL'S FIRST EVANGELIZING TOUR. Churches Founded in Cyprus and Galatia.
		Second Period of Paul's Work in Antioch. Epistle of James.
	50	THE CONFERENCE AT JERUSALEM.
		PAUL'S SECOND EVANGELIZING TOUR. Revisits the Churches of Galatia. Eighteen Months in Corinth. 1 and 2 Thessalonians written there.
		Third Period of Paul's Work in Antioch. Galatians written there.
	55	PAUL'S THIRD EVANGELIZING TOUR. Revisitation in Galatia. Nearly Three Years in Ephesus. 1 Corinthians written there. Revisitation in Macedonia. 2 Corinthians written there. Romans written at Corinth.
		FIFTH VISIT OF PAUL TO JERUSALEM. ARREST AT PENTECOST.
		TRIPLE TRIAL OF PAUL, AND THE CÆSAREAN IMPRISONMENT.
	60	THE VOYAGE TO ROME. SHIPWRECK. WINTER AT MALTA.
		PAUL'S FIRST ROMAN IMPRISONMENT. Colossians, Philemon, Ephesians and Philippians written.
		PERIOD OF PAUL'S RELEASE. Visit to Greece and Asia (possibly also to Spain). 1 Timothy and Titus written.
	65	SUPPOSED SECOND IMPRISONMENT OF PAUL. 2 Timothy. Paul's death (?). Beginning of the Jewish-Roman war. Christians remain neutral.
		Epistles of Peter and Jude written perhaps about this time.
		Gospel of Mark probably written about this time, perhaps in Italy.
		Gospel of Matthew, Epistle to the Hebrews, and the Revelation.
	70	FALL OF JERUSALEM. DESTRUCTION OF THE TEMPLE.
		Gospel of Luke and the Acts probably written somewhere within these ten years, 70-80 A.D.
	80	Johannine Epistles (1, 2, and 3 John) written about this time from Ephesus.
		(Scarce any details of the history 70-100 A.D. are known.)
	90	GOSPEL OF JOHN WRITTEN ABOUT THIS TIME FROM EPHESUS.
		DEATH OF THE APOSTLE JOHN.
	100	CLOSE OF THE PRIMITIVE ERA OF CHRISTIANITY.

Side labels (left margin, spanning regions):
- Throughout Palestine
- Syria and Galatia
- Greece and Asia
- Rome
- All the known world

There is much uncertainty as to the precise dates of the events of the Apostolic Age. The chronology indicated above is that upon which at present there is most agreement among scholars. Much variety of opinion however prevails, and current dates may be still further modified. The consecution of events as recorded in Acts is much more to be trusted, but neither here is there certainty. The relative importance of events is indicated roughly by the relative sizes of type.

THE PRIMITIVE ERA OF CHRISTIANITY

AS RECORDED IN THE ACTS OF THE APOSTLES
30–63 A. D.

OUTLINE OF THE HISTORY.

FIRST DIVISION.—PERIOD OF JEWISH CHRISTIANITY.

Text: Acts 1:1—7:60.   Time: Four Years, 30–33 A. D.   Locality: Jerusalem.
Leaders: Peter and Stephen.

SEC. 1. The Parting Instructions and the Exaltation of Jesus.
Acts 1:1-26.   May, 30 A. D.   Mt. Olivet, Jerusalem.

SEC. 2. Manifestation of Christ's Spiritual Presence and Leadership.
Acts 2:1-47.   May, 30 A. D.   Jerusalem.

SEC. 3. Renewed Hostility of the Jews toward the Christians.
Acts 3:1—4:31.   About 31–32 A. D. Jerusalem.

SEC. 4. Property Relations and Beneficence of the Jerusalem Christians.
Acts 4:32—5:11.   About 31–33 A. D. Jerusalem.

SEC. 5. Apostolic Miracle-Working and Further Jewish Persecution.
Acts 5:12-42.   About 32–33 A. D. Jerusalem.

SEC. 6. First Step in the Development of Christian Organization.
Acts 6:1-7.   About 32-33 A. D. Jerusalem.

SEC. 7. The Preaching of Stephen and its Consequences.
Acts 6:8—7:60.   33 A. D.   Jerusalem.

SECOND DIVISION.—PERIOD OF GOSPEL EXPANSION.

Text: Acts 8:1—15:35.   Time: Seventeen Years, 34-50 A. D.   Localities: Palestine, Syria, Galatia.   Leaders: Peter, James, and Paul.

SEC. 8. First Extension of Organized Christianity beyond Jerusalem.
Acts 8:1-40.   34 A. D.   Samaria and elsewhere.

SEC. 9. The Conversion of Paul from Judaism to Christianity.
Acts 9:1-19a; cf. 22:6-16 and 26:13-18.   34 A. D.   Damascus.

3

FIRST DIVISION.

PERIOD OF JEWISH CHRISTIANITY.

Text: Acts 1 : 1—7 : 60.   Time : Four Years, 30–33 A. D.   Locality : Jerusalem.
Leaders : Peter and Stephen.

During this period the organized Christian community is confined to Jerusalem. It assumes its primitive system of government, rites, methods, and teaching. It becomes firmly established as the Jewish Mother-Church of Christianity. It grows firmly united, and gathers zeal and force for its subsequent missionary activity. It is purified and strengthened by persecution. Its members are Jews, either by birth or by adoption as proselytes. The great problem about which the development of the church during the primitive era turns — namely, whether the Gentiles should be admitted directly to the Christian church without first conforming to Jewish rites — comes into prominence through Stephen only at the close of this period, and serves as the ground of transition to the second period of the history.

Sec. 1. THE PARTING INSTRUCTIONS AND THE EXAL-
TATION OF JESUS.

Acts 1 : 1-26.   May, 30 A. D.   Mt. Olivet, Jerusalem.

I. Study of the Facts.

Let the following subclassification and abstract of the material in this section be verified, corrected, or improved :

Par. 1. 1 : 1-8,   Jesus' Parting Instructions to his Disciples.
Par. 2. 1 : 9-11,   The Ascension of Jesus.
Par. 3. 1 : 12-14, Fellowship of the Waiting Disciples.
Par. 4. 1 : 15-26, Election of Matthias to the Twelve.

Abstract.—The earlier book [Luke's Gospel] narrated the life of Jesus, the present book continues the Christian history from that point. Jesus promised a Spirit baptism to his disciples which should indue them for their work of spreading the gospel through the world. For this they were to wait in Jerusalem. Then from Mt. Olivet came Jesus' exalta-

5

tion to heaven, and the divine assurance of his return. The company of disciples left by Jesus consisted of the eleven faithful apostles, certain devoted Galilean women with Jesus' mother, the now believing brethren of Jesus, and others, to the number of 120. At one of their meetings Peter, as spokesman of the company, suggested that the vacancy in the twelve made by the withdrawal of Judas be filled. The new apostle must be one who had witnessed Jesus' entire ministry and resurrection. Of two of their number thus qualified one, Matthias, was chosen by lot—a means of determining the divine choice.

II. Topics for Investigation.

1. *The last instructions of Jesus.*—With whom was Jesus assembled (vs. 4), where, when, and for what purpose ? What was the promise of the Father (vs. 4) for which Jesus directed them to wait (*cf.* Luke 24: 49; John 7: 39; 16: 7–14)? Why was a waiting period necessary, how long was it to be, and why in Jerusalem ? Does vs. 4 indicate that Jesus' disciples had been baptized by John ? Could it be understood from vs. 5 that water baptism was of the old dispensation (*cf.* Matt. 11:11), but that in the new dispensation it was replaced by the baptism of the Spirit (*cf.* Acts 19:1–6)? Compare the water baptism of John with the Spirit baptism promised here. Who were come together (vs. 6), where, when, and why ? What power were they to receive (vs. 8), and how was it different from the power they already had ? What commission (vs. 8) did Jesus give the disciples ? Compare with this Matt. 28:18–20; Luke 24:47–49. What was the scope of this mission ? Did the disciples so understand it from the first and attempt to carry it out ? Of what were they to be witnesses (vs. 8)? See the passages where such witness-bearing is recorded, Luke 24:53; Acts 2:32; 10:37–43; 13:23–31, and others. What qualifications in this matter were requisite for apostles (vss. 21, 22)?

2. *The apostles' idea of the kingdom.*—What suggested this question (vs. 6) which the disciples addressed to Jesus ? What did they mean by the restoration of the kingdom to Israel ? To what extent did the disciples still expect Jesus to become a political, temporal, and visible Messiah ? How could they hold these views after receiving Jesus' teaching of the spiritual Messiahship ? Consider Jesus' reply to their question. To what event or events did Jesus refer, the "times and seasons" of which had not been disclosed (*cf.* Mark 13:32)? Explain the patience of Jesus in dealing with the lingering misconceptions of himself and his work.

3. *The exaltation of Jesus.*—Compare the other accounts of the ascension in Mark 16:19, 20; Luke 24:50, 51. Compare with it also the translation of Elijah, 2 Kings 2:9–12. What is meant (vs. 9) by "taken up"? What was the cloud which received him (*cf.* Mark 9:7; 1 Kings 8:10, 11; Isaiah 6:1–4)? What was the purpose of God in this visible exaltation of his Son? Who were the two white-robed men (*cf.* Luke 24:1–7), and why were they present? What prompted their question to the disciples? Just what information did they give? What is to be understood by the statement that "in like manner" Jesus will return (*cf.* the same phrase in Matt. 23:37; Luke 13:34; Acts 7:28; and see Matt. 24:30; Mark 13:26)? Compare the angelic appearance of vss. 10, 11 with other angelic appearances recounted by Luke (*e. g.*, Luke 1:11–22, 26–38; 2:8–15; 22:43; 24:4–8; Acts 7:30–38; 10:3–7; 12:7–15), as also with similar accounts in other gospels (Matt. 1:20–24; 2:13–21; 28:2–7; John 12:29; 20:12, 13); what view should be taken as to the reality and as to the details of these manifestations?

4. *The first group of disciples.*—Observe four different elements which constituted this primitive company of Christians: *a*) The eleven apostles; compare this list (vs. 13) with those found in Matt. 10:2–4; Mark 3:16–19; Luke 6:14–16. *b*) Jesus' mother and other women who had been adherents of Jesus in his public ministry (*cf.* Mark 15:40; Luke 8:1–3; 23:49; 24:22; Acts 8:3). *c*) Jesus' own brothers; how many, what change had taken place in them, and why (*cf.* Matt. 13:55; John 7:3–5; 1 Cor. 15:7)? *d*) Other unnamed disciples, making in all 120 (vs. 15). Where were the homes of these followers of Christ? Were there still other disciples elsewhere (*cf.* 1 Cor. 15:6)? Why was the number of the Christians so small? How was this company engaged during the waiting period?

5. *The election of Matthias to the twelve.*—Why did Peter suggest that the place left vacant by Judas should be filled? Are vss. 18, 19 to be regarded as the words of Peter, or as a parenthetic addition of the writer or his source? How is this account of Judas' death to be explained in view of the account contained in Matt. 26:47–50? Was it God's will that Judas' place in the twelve should be filled; if so, what of the view that Paul was divinely intended to take the place rather than Matthias? Whence did Luke, who was not one of this company, derive the information contained in this chapter? Ascertain the meaning in their original historical setting of the Old Testament passages cited by Peter in support of his suggestion, Ps. 69:25;

109:8. Consider the use made of them in this connection by Peter. Since both Matthias and Barsabbas were qualified for the apostolate, why did not the disciples themselves select the one or the other? What use was accustomed to be made of the lot, and how was it operated? Was the lot a proper mode of ascertaining the divine will? Was the divine choice limited to one of the two named? By the term "Lord" (vs. 24) is God to be understood, or Christ? Do we know anything further about Matthias or Barsabbas? In this first recorded business meeting of the disciples, were the apostles shown to be officers, or merely leaders, Peter acting as spokesman of the group? Did the whole company take equal part in the business which was transacted? Was the method of procedure entirely democratic? Is there any evidence of formal officers or of any formal organization of the Christians at this time?

III.   OBSERVATIONS AND TEACHINGS.

Under this head the more important facts and teachings of this chapter are to be gathered and arranged topically, so that the great lines of the history shall clearly appear, as well as its practical bearing upon our own lives. The observations and teachings which follow are only by way of suggestion. They should be traced to their sources in Acts 1 and verified or corrected. Then others should be added to them which the student will find. The permanent value of the study will be much increased by faithful work at this point.

1. *Organization.*—The Jerusalem group of Christians numbered 120, and there were perhaps some others elsewhere; but Jesus' work had not had numerical success.—It was regarded as important that the place in the twelve left vacant by Judas' withdrawal should be filled from the body of disciples, and Matthias was appointed to the apostolate.—There was as yet no formal organization of the Christians; the apostles acted as leaders, and Peter was the spokesman of the company.—The disciples, in the transaction of their business, seem to have acted upon thoroughly democratic principles.

2. *Environment.*—The ten days of this period were spent quietly by the Christians, without aggressive work, waiting for the fulfilment of Christ's promise.—The Jewish enemies were inactive after the culmination of their persecution in the death of Jesus.—Jesus plainly pointed out the whole world as the sphere of the gospel; to his conception it was a universal religion.—The brothers of Jesus, who disbelieved in his claims during his life, became his followers after his resurrection.—The believing women were a testimony to the fact that the gospel had placed woman on a higher, freer, and better plane.

3. *Institutions.*—The rites of baptism and the Lord's Supper are not yet mentioned, but were probably recognized, for on the day of

Pentecost they appear in the records.—The Christians had meetings for worship and prayer.—They probably continued also the observance of Jewish religious customs.

4. *Belief and teaching.*—Christ's resurrection appearances and teaching were all-important in the preparation of the disciples for their work.—Jesus dealt gently with the Messianic misconception which still remained in the apostles' minds.—The departure of the visible Christ was accompanied by the assurance of his return.—Jesus gave no answer concerning the time of his return, since he himself did not know when it would be and did not consider it of importance to know.—New experiences led to a new understanding and use of the Old Testament Scriptures which contained types and foreshadowings of the Messianic period.

5. *Daily life.*—The injunctions of Christ were faithfully kept by his disciples.—The early Christians were closely united both in their social and in their religious life.—They awaited the fulfilment of the promise with trust, thanksgiving, joy, and expectancy.

6. *Divine guidance.*—Jesus' parting command and promise show his continued relation, beyond the ascension, to his followers on earth. —The Holy Spirit was to be always with them in full measure to guide and strengthen them in their work.—Devotion, ability, and energy in a few persons counted for more than numbers in spreading and establishing the gospel.

Literature.—This section of Acts receives elucidation in all the commentaries on Acts, under Chap. I; see the commentaries of GLOAG (Scribners, N. Y., 2 vols., $7.00), HACKETT (Amer. Bapt. Pub. Society, Philadelphia, $2.00), MEYER (Funk & Wagnalls Co., N. Y., $3.00), CAMBRIDGE BIBLE (Macmillan Co., N. Y., $1.10), and others. These are all first-class works. Gloag's Commentary is the best, but expensive. Next to it stands Hackett's. Meyer's Commentary, of high value, would hardly be satisfactory if only one commentary could be afforded. The Cambridge Bible will be found sufficient for most students. The general works upon the Apostolic Age make little or no reference to this portion of the history, but see McGIFFERT, History of Christianity in the Apostolic Age (Scribners, N. Y., $2.50), pp. 36–48.

SEC. 2. MANIFESTATION OF CHRIST'S SPIRITUAL PRES-
ENCE AND LEADERSHIP.

Acts 2 : 1-47.   May, 30 A. D.   Jerusalem.

I. STUDY OF THE FACTS.

Let the following subclassification and abstract of the material in
this section be verified, corrected, or improved :

Par. 1. 2 : 1-4,   Fulfilment of the Promise of the Spirit.
Par. 2. 2 : 5-13,   The Inspired Tongue-speaking.
Par. 3. 2 : 14-36, Peter's Pentecostal Address.
Par. 4. 2 : 37-42, Numerical Increase of the Christians.
Par. 5. 2 : 43-47, The Disciples' Manner of Life.

Abstract.—On the day of Pentecost following the ascension, while
the disciples were assembled in a private house for prayer, the promised outpouring of the Spirit came, attested to the senses by accom-
panying noise and symbolic light, as also by tongue-speaking among
the Christians. The strange sound attracted to the place where the
disciples were assembled a large number of Jews and Jewish proselytes,
some of them residents in Jerusalem, others from foreign lands sojourning in the city in attendance upon the feast. All wished to know the
meaning of this remarkable occurrence. The apostles, through their
spokesman Peter, gave the explanation. They were witnessing the
fulfilment of Joel's prediction that at the coming of the Messiah's kingdom God would pour out his Spirit so abundantly that all would
prophesy. The Messiah had come in the person of Jesus of Nazareth,
whose wonderful works attested his divine mission. He had been
rejected and crucified, but that had been foreseen and foreordained
by God, who had now exalted him. The psalmist had predicted how
the Messiah should be released from the grave and should sit at God's
right hand. This had taken place, Jesus had been made Lord of all,
and his kingdom was now being conspicuously established upon the
earth. The effect of the divine manifestation and the apostle's words
was immediate and great. About three thousand persons accepted
Jesus as Messiah and Master, and became associated with the original
body of disciples, receiving from the apostles instruction concerning
the life and teachings of Christ. The Christian community held fast

together, giving to the needy, continuing their Jewish worship, observing the memorial supper of their Lord, living in joy and peace, and
continually winning additions to their number.

II. TOPICS FOR INVESTIGATION.

1. *The Pentecostal coming of the Spirit.*—When and what was the
Jewish feast of Pentecost? *Cf.* Ex. 23 : 14–17 ; Deut. 16 : 1–17.   Did
Pentecost in the year 30 A. D. fall upon the first day of the week
(Sunday)?   Why was the day of Pentecost chosen by God for the out-
pouring of the Spirit ?   How long was this after the resurrection, and
after the ascension, of Jesus ?   Recall Jesus' promise of the Spirit, *cf.*
Acts 1 : 4, 5 ; John 15 : 26 ; 16 : 7–14.   Had not the Holy Spirit
been present and active among men before this time ?   What was the
peculiarity of this Pentecostal visitation ?   Was this bestowal in part of
temporary gifts, *e. g.*, tongue-speaking and miracle-working ?   Where
were the Christians assembled on this day, and for what purpose ?
On the symbolic wind and fire compare Ps. 104 : 3, 4 ; Ezek. 1 : 4 ; Ex.
13 : 21 ; 19 : 16–20.   What was the purpose of these external signs ?

2. *The Jews of the Dispersion.*—In what numbers and where outside
of Palestine were Jews found in the first century A. D.?   Recall the
three great compulsory dispersions of the Jews in the previous centuries,
cf. 2 Kings 15 : 29 ; 17 : 6 ; 25 : 8–11.   Had there also been voluntary
removals of Jews to foreign lands for the pursuit of business?   Why
and how did the dispersed Jews maintain their Jewish religion in the
foreign countries where they dwelt?   In vs. 5 does "dwelling at Jerusalem" mean resident there or sojourning there at the feast, or does it
include both?   Was the feast of Pentecost largely attended by the
Jews of the Dispersion ; if so, why?   Locate upon the map the various
places referred to in vss. 9–11.   Why do these visitors figure so largely
in the account of this Christian occasion?   How did the Jewish Dispersion assist in the spread of the gospel through Gentile lands?

3. *The gift of tongues.*—What is to be inferred from vss. 4, 6, 11,
as to the nature of the tongue-speaking referred to?   Consider two
explanations : an actual speaking in different foreign languages and
dialects, or an ecstatic, incoherent utterance of the believing Christian
manifesting his joy in the possession of the Spirit.   Would the former
gift be necessary in view of the fact that Greek was the common language of all the Roman Empire?   If the apostles were speaking intel-
ligibly in foreign languages why were they by some regarded as drunk
(vs. 13)?   Observe that there was among the primitive Christians a

spiritual gift called tongue-speaking which was uniformly of the second character described above, *cf.* Acts 10:46; 19:6; 1 Cor. 12–14 (esp. 14:14, 19, 22, 23).   May it be, then, that the source from which Luke drew his account of the day of Pentecost misunderstood the phenomenon, and that it was in fact only the common tongue-speaking? See especially Schaff's *History of the Christian Church*, Vol. I, pp. 231–242.

4. *Peter's Pentecostal discourse.*—Why did Peter give the address on this occasion? Why did the eleven apostles stand up with him? What two classes of people did he designate among his hearers? Was it the main point of Peter's discourse to prove to the Jews that Jesus was the Messiah in spite of his humiliation and death? Consider carefully the steps of his argument to this end. Under what circumstances was this quoted prophecy of Joel (2:28–32) originally given? Explain the use made of it by Peter in this connection. What is meant (vs. 17) by the "last days"? What is meant (vs. 20) by the "day of the Lord"? Consider the original historical meaning of Ps. 16:8–11 quoted in this address. What argument did Peter deduce from it, and was his interpretation of the passage valid? What was Peter's argument from Ps. 110:1 for the exaltation of Christ, *cf.* Matt. 22:43–45? Consider in detail the points of teaching about Christ contained in the discourse. Show how the discourse was adapted to the situation. What was its effect? From what classes came the new converts? What was required of them? Account for the large number of converts. Why had not Jesus had such numerical success? How did Luke probably obtain this account of the day of Pentecost for his history? Are we to suppose that all of Peter's discourse is here recorded, or that we have only the main points he made, the substance of what he said?

5. *Characteristics of the primitive Christian life.*—What were the conditions of entrance (belief, conduct, and form) to the company of disciples? What had made baptism a Christian rite, *cf.* Luke 24:47; Matt. 28:19? What did baptism signify to these converts, and how was it administered? Was there also a Spirit baptism, *cf.* Acts 1:5; 2:28; 19:1–6? Was the Lord's Supper also observed as a Christian rite ("breaking of bread," *cf.* Acts 20:7, 11; 1 Cor. 10:16), and why, *cf.* Matt. 26:26–29; Luke 22:14–20? What was the apostles' teaching to which the new disciples gave continued attention (vs. 42)—was it instruction in the life and teaching of Jesus? What wonders and signs were done by the apostles (vs. 43), and why? Consider the self-sacri-

fice and charity of the primitive Christians as described in vss. 44, 45. Why did the Christians, who at this time were practically all Jews, remain faithful to the temple service and Jewish worship generally? Had Christ taught that Christianity was independent of Judaism? If so, why did they not so believe and act? Did they have also distinctly Christian meetings for prayer, worship, and fellowship? Account for the unity, joy, and praise of this Christian company. Explain the meaning of vs. 47, last clause. Compare this type of Christian living with ours of the present day, showing points of excellence and of deficiency in each.

III. OBSERVATIONS AND TEACHINGS.

1. *Organization.*— There is still no formal organization of the Christians, although the number is greatly increased; but a close fellowship and united activity and life.—The Christians were gathered together for united worship when the great outpouring of the Spirit came.—The apostles stood up to represent the body of the disciples, while Peter spoke as the representative of the apostles.— Peter here sustains the same relation to the other apostles as during Christ's ministry—he is leader and spokesman.

2. *Environment.*—The time had come when Christianity could achieve numerical success.—The large number of new disciples were mostly visitors to the feast from Galilee and foreign lands.—They were almost wholly Jews, with perhaps some Gentiles who had become Jews by adopting that religion.— It may be presumed that the chief persecutors of Jesus were not among the converts.

3. *Institutions.*— Baptism was used as a symbolic rite of entrance upon the Christian life; it seems to have been instituted by Jesus, although he did not himself use it in his work.—The breaking of bread (Lord's Supper) was observed as a memorial of Christ, in accordance with his instruction; it took place either at the beginning or at the end of a common Christian meal daily.—The Christians adhered to their Jewish worship; at the same time they had distinctly Christian meetings for prayer, worship, and fellowship.

4. *Belief and teaching.*— Peter's discourse is full of truth newly conceived and presented, and is manifestly inspired utterance.—The main teaching of the discourse is that Jesus is Messiah and Lord, a truth witnessed to by his work on earth, and especially by the Old Testament Messianic prophecies which found their fulfilment in him. —The emphasis is here laid on the prophecies because he was address-

ing Jews who believed in these.— Peter explained the humiliation, rejection, and death of Christ as foreseen by God rather than a thwarting of his purposes, and showed how his resurrection and exaltation removed that objection to believing in him.— Repentance, and baptism as a symbol of it, were necessary to an acceptance of Christ and a fellowship with his disciples.— Instruction in the facts and the truths of the gospel formed an essential part in the daily life of the Christians.

5. *Daily life.*— Besides the instruction just referred to, the daily life of the Christians was marked by close association, unity of heart and action, joy, worship, and prayer, commemoration of Christ, and energetic preaching of the gospel.— The Christian life, work, and teaching impressed and won the unconverted about them, so that their numbers continually increased.— It is not known whether the Christians stopped their common avocations in order to give their whole time to the new life and activity ; probably some of them did so ; at any rate they had frequent meetings at private houses and were faithful and earnest in their evangelical work.

6. *Divine guidance.*— Christ's relations to his people are vital and permanent.—The Holy Spirit is present in believers, and in the world, to carry forward the kingdom which Christ established.—The inner experience of the Spirit was signified and emphasized on the day of Pentecost by external symbolic manifestations.—The opportunity given the Christians to reach the multitude with the gospel was fully used.

Literature.— Full treatment of this important section of Acts will be found in all commentaries on the book ; see especially GLOAG, HACKETT, MEYER, and the CAMBRIDGE BIBLE.   Many other works also treat of this event, only the more important of which (and such as are in English) will be mentioned : MCGIFFERT, History of Christanity in the Apostolic Age, pp. 48-74 ; WEIZSÄCKER, Apostolic Age of the Christian Church (Putnam's Sons, N. Y., 2 vols., $7), Vol. I, chaps. ii and iii ; RAMSAY, St. Paul the Traveler (Putnam's Sons, N. Y., $3), pp. 363-365 ; SCHAFF, History of the Christian Church (Scribners, N. Y., $4), Vol. 1, pp. 225-245 ; NEANDER, Planting and Training of the Christian Church (Macmillan Co., N. Y., 2 vols., $2), Vol. I, pp. 3-23, Vol. II, pp. 58-64 ; FARRAR, Life and Work of St. Paul (Dutton & Co., N. Y., $2), chaps. v and vii ; STIFLER, Introduction to the Book of Acts (Revell Co., Chicago, $0.75), secs. ii and iii.

SEC. 3.   RENEWED HOSTILITY OF THE JEWS TOWARD THE CHRISTIANS.

Acts 3:1—4:31.   About 31-32 A. D.   Jerusalem.

I. STUDY OF THE FACTS.

Let the following subclassification and abstract of the material in this section be verified, corrected, or improved :

Par. 1. 3:1-11, A Miracle of Healing by the Apostles.
Par. 2. 3:12-26, Peter's Subsequent Discourse in Solomon's Porch.
Par. 3. 4:1-4, The Arrest of Peter and John by the Jews.
Par. 4. 4:5-12, Their Trial before the Sanhedrin.
Par. 5. 4:13-22, The Unwilling Release of the Apostles.
Par. 6. 4:23-31, Consequent Thanksgiving and Prayer of the Christians.

Abstract.— On one occasion, as Peter and John were going into the temple to pray, they came upon a lame beggar, and partly for his own sake, partly to attract the attention of the people that they might preach the gospel to them, they healed the man.   Then Peter declared to the throng of people that this cure which had amazed them was wrought by God, through Jesus their Messiah whom they had put to death, but whom God had raised and exalted to heaven. And if they would now repent of all their sins, Christ would return, and the great Messianic era would come.   The Jews, particularly the Sadducees, hated and feared the Christian movement.   Therefore Peter and John were arrested and brought to trial before the Sanhedrin.   Nothing could be done, however, for the cure could not be denied, and the popular favor toward the apostles was strong.   They were simply dismissed with the charge that they should stop preaching the gospel, a thing which Peter and John refused to do.   The Christians were greatly rejoiced at this victory, and gave themselves with new courage to their work of spreading the gospel.

II. TOPICS FOR INVESTIGATION.

1. *The cure and its significance.*—What is the relation of this incident to Acts 2:43 ?   Can the time of it be ascertained ?   Describe the condition of the cripple (*cf.* Acts 3:2, 10; 4:22).   Did he know

that Peter and John were Christian apostles? Exactly what did Peter mean by his words "Silver and gold have I none"? Why did he heal this lame beggar? Explain the significance of Peter's command, "In the name of Jesus Christ of Nazareth, walk." Observe that the cure was witnessed by many (cf. Acts 3:9; 4:16). See the account in Acts 14:8-18 of a similar cure worked by Paul. What reasons were there for recording this miracle at such length?

2. *Peter's discourse in the temple.*—Describe the circumstances under which Peter spoke these words (3:12-26) to the people. Recall Christ's discourse here at the temple a year or two before (cf. John 10:22-42). Had the activities of the Christians during this intervening period been mainly confined to their own company and life, or had they been publicly preaching and working? State the line of thought which Peter followed in his address. What were the chief points of truth which he brought out? Review in the gospel accounts the facts about Jesus which Peter adduces in 3:13-15. On the term "Servant" (3:13, 26) compare Isa. 42:1; Matt. 12:18; Acts 4:27, 30. Explain Peter's statement (vs. 17) that the Jews had through ignorance crucified Jesus. Why did Peter declare that God had foreseen what would happen to Christ, and in it his purpose had been fulfilled (cf. also Acts 2:23; Luke 22:22; 1 Cor. 1:23)? Explain the phrase (vs. 21) "the times of restoration of all things" (cf. Isa. 1:24-27; Matt. 17:11; Acts 1:26; Rom. 8:22, 23; 1 Cor. 15:19-28). Compare carefully the Old Testament quotation in vss. 22, 23 with the original in Deut. 18:15-19. Was the reference there to an individual Messiah, or to a line of prophets? State from 3:26 the nature of the blessing which Christ brought to men. What was the practical aim of this discourse? Was its purpose accomplished? How are we to understand that this account of the discourse was handed down? Have we all that Peter said at the time, or only the substance of his address? What is the value to us of this record?

3. *The trial and release of the apostles.*—Why had there been no persecution of the Christians since the crucifixion until this time? How had the Christian community been progressing since that time? State the way in which this persecution arose. Who were the leaders in this opposition (4:1)? Why were the Sadducees now aroused against the Christians? Did the Pharisees also join in the movement? Explain the fact that the chief enemies of Christ were the Pharisees, while the chief enemies of his followers were, during this period, the Sadducees. What does the full, formal meeting of the

Sanhedrin indicate as to the nature of this trial ?   What charge was made against Peter and John ?   Were they subject to the authority of the Sanhedrin ?   Consider carefully the defense which Peter made. Explain in detail the meaning of 4:12 (*cf.* John 3:18; 14:6; 1 Cor. 3:11; Gal. 1:8, 9; Phil. 2:9–11; Heb. 2:3).   What was the decision of the Sanhedrin in this case ?   Why was it so mild (*cf.* 4:16, 21)? Did the apostles submit to the decision ?

4.   *Peter and John, leading apostles.*—Why were these two men so closely associated in Christian work (*cf.* Mark 6:7; Luke 22:8; John 1:41; 18:16; 20:6; Acts 8:14; Gal. 2:9)?   Should we understand from Acts 3 and 4 that John was always silent in public, or that he also spoke to the people and before the Sanhedrin, but that his words have not been preserved ?   If the latter, why were they not preserved ? What is the meaning of "unlearned and ignorant" as applied in 4:13 to Peter and John?   Does it refer to the fact that they had not been trained in the Jewish rabbinical schools (*cf.* John 7:15)?   As a matter of fact, are the indications strong, both from their work and their writings, that Peter and John were well educated (for their time and country), and were possessed of peculiar ability ?   Is our English translation of this passage misleading therefore?   What is the meaning of the phrase "took knowledge" in 4:13 (*cf.* 3:10)?   Also, what is the meaning of the phrase "been with Jesus" in the same verse; does it indicate anything more than that they had been formerly seen in company with Jesus (*cf.* Mark 14:66–71)?

5.   *Thanksgiving and prayer of the Christians.*—Was the outcome of this trial a victory for the Christians over their bitterest opponents? Explain why this was an important crisis for the gospel.   What were the several reasons for this triumph of the gospel?   What was the number of the Christians at this time (*cf.* 4:4)?   How did they hear of the result of the trial?   Was prayer the most natural expression of their joy?   Consider carefully what is contained in the prayer here recorded : ascription to God (vs. 24), recalling the prophecy (vss. 25, 26), description of the situation (vss. 27, 28), appeal to God for pro-tection, courage, assistance, testimony (vss. 29, 30).   Why was this prayer addressed to God rather than to Christ?   What is the New Testament usage in this matter?   Compare the Old Testament quota-tion (vss. 25, 26) with the original in Ps. 2:1, 2.   How did it apply to this situation of the Christians?   With the facts and teachings con-tained in verses 27 and 28 compare the gospel records on these points. For what did the Christians now pray (vss. 29, 30)?   In what ways

was their prayer answered? As to the form of this prayer, was it a prayer made on the occasion by one of the disciples, in which all joined; or was it a stated prayer or chant of the Christians, already familiar from use on other occasions, which the Christians now repeated?

III.   OBSERVATIONS AND TEACHINGS.

1. *Organization.*—The whole number of Christians at this time in Jerusalem is recorded as about five thousand.—There is still no formal organization of the Christians, the apostles acting as the leaders of the community.— Peter and John, often before associated together, appear in this section as public preachers of the gospel, and as conspicuous representatives of the Christian movement are brought to trial before the Sanhedrin.—The disciples were closely bound together in love for one another and devotion to the gospel.

2. *Environment.*—A year or two after the crucifixion of Jesus there arose another persecution of Christianity by the Jews.— In this persecution the lead was taken by the Sadducees, for they feared that the Christians would gain the support of the people and then set up a revolt against Roman authority which would overthrow the Sadducean political control and rob the Jews of what freedom they had (*cf.* John 11:47-49).—The Pharisees did not join actively in this persecution because the Christians, contrary to the example of Jesus, did not antagonize the Pharisaic system, but continued their conformity to established Jewish rites and customs along with their Christianity.— The people were friendly to the Christians, and restrained the Sanhedrin from violence against Peter and John.

3. *Institutions.*—As just stated, the Christians remained faithful to the religious observances of Judaism, and here the two apostles appear in attendance upon one of the prayer hours at the temple.— A gathering of the Christians for united thanksgiving and prayer followed the release of Peter and John.— It is possible that in this connection we have a liturgical fragment, indicating that even so early the Christians had set forms of prayer; this explanation of the prayer is suggested by the absence from it of any specific references to this situation, the words being so general that they might refer to any of their escapes from Jewish persecution.

4. *Belief and teaching.*—It was the God of Israel who had been manifested in and was now working through Christ.— Peter charged the Jews with the murder of Jesus, but explained their action as due to ignorance.— Now, at any rate, they could be no longer ignorant of

the Messiahship of Jesus, because of his resurrection.—They should all repent, then their sins would be forgiven, and Christ would come again to consummate his kingdom.—God sent Christ to bless men by turning them from their iniquities.—It is only in and through Christ that salvation has come to men.—There is an authority higher than any human authority, to which all men owe supreme allegiance.

5. *Daily life.*—Miracles were worked by the apostles, but only and confessedly in the name and by the power of Jesus.—It is the privilege of the poor in this world to make many rich, and having nothing yet to possess all things.—Peter and John, going about their daily duties, took the opportunity to restore a cripple and to preach the gospel with marvelous power and effect to a large number who were interested by the cure. —The Christian company were gathered together awaiting in suspense the outcome of the trial of the apostles, showing their loving union.

6. *Divine guidance.*—Peter and John were by the grace of God courageous, confident, and independent before the Sanhedrin.—By divine providence the popular sentiment of sympathy for the Christians was so strong that the Jewish rulers did not dare to do the apostles harm.—The grace, inspiration, and assistance needed by the disciples were constantly given them by God.

Literature.—There will be little found upon this section outside of the commentaries on Acts, see those of GLOAG, HACKETT, MEYER, and the CAMBRIDGE BIBLE. Also McGIFFERT, History of Christianity in the Apostolic Age, pp. 74–76; NEANDER, Planting and Training of the Christian Church, Vol. I, pp. 41–46; STIFLER, Introduction to the Book of Acts, sec. iv. Information upon the text can often be obtained by the use of a Bible dictionary; the best at present is SMITH'S BIBLE DICTIONARY, second edition (Christian Literature Co., N. Y., 3 vols., $22); a new Bible dictionary is being prepared by Messrs. T. & T. Clark of Edinburgh (Scribners, N. Y., importers), in four volumes, the first of which was published in 1898; and still another, of smaller size, is being prepared by Messrs. A. & C. Black of London (Macmillan Co., N. Y., importers), in two volumes, to appear within a year or two. That published by the Clarks will probably be the best of the three for general use.

PROPERTY RELATIONS AND BENEFICENCE OF
THE JERUSALEM CHRISTIANS.

Acts 4 : 32—5 : 11.   About 31–33 A. D.   Jerusalem.

I. Study of the Facts.

Let the following subclassification and abstract of the material in
this section be verified, corrected, or improved:

Par. 1. 4:32–35, Unity of Heart and Community of Goods.

Par. 2. 4:36, 37, Barnabas' Notable Gift.

Par. 3. 5:1–11, The Sin and Punishment of Ananias and Sapphira.

Abstract.—The Christians were one in heart, interest, and possessions. The Holy Spirit was with them in their ministry to unbelievers
and to each other. A charity fund for the poorer brethren was pro-
vided by those who had more wealth. Particularly interesting was the
generous contribution of Barnabas, whose home was in distant Cyprus.
One sad instance marred this enthusiastic beneficence. Two members
of the brotherhood, who wished to appear as generous as the others,
but who were at heart wholly selfish, in hypocrisy offered a contribution. This sin struck so vitally at the integrity and purity of the
Christian community that it called down divine judgment upon them.
Under Peter's condemnation, first Ananias and later his wife were visited by sudden death. A deep feeling of awe came over all at this
solemn, severe meting out of divine justice for the purification of the
body of disciples from its unholy members.

II. Topics for Investigation.

1. *The common life of the Christians.*— Do vss. 32–35 give a brief
general description of the Christian community in these first years of
its life? Explain the meaning of the phrase "of one heart and soul"
(vs. 32 ; *cf.* 1 Chron. 12:38; Jer. 32:39; Rom. 15:5, 6; Phil. 2:2;
1 Peter 3:8). About what was the number of Christians in Jerusalem at
this time (*cf.* Acts 4:4)? What reasons were there for this great harmony of feeling and activity? Observe once more that witness-bearing
to the resurrection of Christ was one of the chief features of their work
(*cf.* Acts 1:8, 22; 2:32; 3:15; 4:10). Compare the title "Lord Jesus"
in vs. 33 with other designations of Christ in Acts (1:1, 14, 21; 2:22,
32, 36; 3:6, 13-15, 18, 20, 26; 4:2, 10, 13, 18, 27, 30). Meaning of

"great grace was upon them all" (vs. 33)? How did the fraternity of
the disciples appear in their property relations? Is the expression
"laid them at the apostles' feet" (vs. 35, *cf.* vs. 37 and 5:2) to be
understood literally or figuratively? Why had the apostles given a
surname (vs. 36) to Joseph? Why is it mentioned that Barnabas was
a Levite? Locate Cyprus upon the map; was Barnabas' home there?
Describe the spiritual and moral condition of the community in general. Does Peter still appear as the leading disciple? Were there yet
any formal officers among the Christians? In 5:11 the term "church"
is for the first time in Acts used of the body of Christians; what is the
significance of this? When did this term, as an historical fact, begin
to be used in this way? What terms had been used of the Christians
up to this time (*cf.* Acts 1:15, 16; 4:23, 32)?

2. *The sharing of goods at Jerusalem.*—Make a careful study of
Acts 2:44, 45; 4:32, 34; 5:4, to determine the exact nature of this
sharing of goods among the Jerusalem Christians. How much need
was there for such charity? What were the causes of this poverty
among the disciples? What kind of property was disposed of for these
purposes? Why is Barnabas' gift especially mentioned (vss. 36, 37)?
Was this sharing of goods required, or was it in every case purely voluntary? Did those who contributed give all they had, or only such
a proportion as they saw fit? Was the private ownership of property
abolished, or was it simply a high degree of the sharing of goods
between those Christians who had abundance and those who were in
need? What were the underlying causes of this arrangement: (*a*) fra-
ternal beneficence toward needy brethren; or (*b*) the supposition that
it was instituted and approved by Christ in the case of himself and his
apostles, and should therefore be continued among his followers; or
(*c*) the anticipation of Christ's speedy return, when earthly possessions
would no longer be of value? Was there any relation between this
Christian sharing of goods and the communism of the Essenes of the
time (*cf.* Josephus' *Wars of the Jews*, II, 8, 3)? How long did this
state of things continue among the Jerusalem Christians? Is there any
further reference to it in the Acts or epistles? Was it ever tried elsewhere; if not, why not? Was it a success or a failure at Jerusalem?
Can any argument for communism among Christians be drawn from
this sharing of goods?

3. *The sin of Ananias and Sapphira.*—Were they members of the
Christian community? Is anything known about them beyond what
is here recorded? What was it that they did? Why did they keep

back part of the price? Were they under any obligations to give it all
cf. vs. 4)? Did their sin lie in their hypocritical pretense that the
amount turned over to the brotherhood was the whole amount received?
Why did they make such a misrepresentation? Was it deliberately
planned? Were Ananias and Sapphira equal partakers in the decep-
tion? May their sin be described as a "spurious imitation of exalted
virtue"? How did Peter know of their hypocrisy? Were they at
heart selfish, while at the same time they wished to *appear* as generous
as the others? Explain the meaning (vs. 3) of "Satan filled thy heart."
What was it (vs. 3) to "lie to the Holy Ghost"? In connection with
vs. 6 ascertain something about the burial customs of the time. What
is the meaning (vs. 9) of the phrase "to tempt the Spirit of the Lord"?

4. *Justification of the divine punishment.*— In the founding of a
great institution, such as was the Christian church, is it essential to
have the principles of that institution absolutely recognized and established at the outset? To secure this, what degree of resistance to
enemies of the institution will be justifiable? Could any blow be more
dangerous to the infant church than one aimed at the purity and sincerity of the moral and religious life of its members? Was the sin of
Ananias and Sapphira anything less than this? Consider whether it
was premeditated, grossly corrupting, from within the body of believers,
and essentially unchristian. What sort of punishment in this case would
(*a*) extirpate selfishness and hypocrisy from the Christian community,
(*b*) exclude all who were not genuine Christians, and (*c*) support the
divine authority of the apostles in the founding of the Christian
church? Was anything short of the punishment inflicted upon Ananias and Sapphira adequate to effect these things? Did the punishment in fact accomplish these things? Consider similar visitations of
God upon sin at critical points in religious development as recorded
in the Old Testament (*cf.* Gen. 4 : 1–15 ; Lev. 10 : 1–7 ; Num. 16 : 1–35 ;
Josh. 7 : 1–26 ; 2 Sam. 6 : 1–7). Is there reason to think, with Professor
Ramsay,[1] that the account of the Ananias and Sapphira incident has
been so modified in transmission as not now to represent exactly what
took place?

III.   Observations and Teachings.

1. *Organization.*— Again Peter appears as leader and spokesman of
the Christian community.—The apostles were at this time the over-

[1] *St. Paul the Traveler*, p. 370 : "The episode of Ananias and Sapphira (5 : 1–11)
excites reasonable suspicion. . . . . The desire to bring into strong relief the
unselfishness of the primitive church has worked itself out in a moral apologue which
has found here an entrance alongside of real history."

seers of the distribution of the charitable funds among the Christians. —The disciples were united in one happy company, of one heart and soul, sharing their goods and preaching the gospel.—Two unworthy members of the community were removed by divine visitation.

2. *Environment.*—The Christians were now at rest from persecution from without.—But the purity and integrity of the body of disciples was threatened from within, by the hypocrisy and falsehood of two members of the community.—Christianity produced a profound impression upon those who witnessed it.

3. *Institutions.*—It does not appear that the sharing of goods among the Jerusalem Christians was a communistic condition.—For this sharing was voluntary, limited, local and temporary, and did not go beyond a high degree of generosity in giving to their brethren according to their needs.—It may be inferred that the judgment upon Ananias and Sapphira came upon them in a public meeting of the Christians.

4. *Belief and teaching.*—All sin is primarily against God.—The desire to appear what one is not, coveting a reputation for doing what one does not do, and the simulation of a feeling which one does not feel, are nothing less than hypocrisy, which is essentially unchristian and subversive of that which is right and good.—The extreme punishment visited upon Ananias and Sapphira was held to be just and necessary to the well-being of the community.

5. *Daily life.*—It would seem that in some respects there was ideal fellowship, sympathy, and generosity among the Christians at this time.—They were one in heart, purpose, and life.—Their great work was the spread of the gospel by witnessing to the resurrection, and therefore the living lordship of Christ.—A shadow had fallen across the community in the great sin of two of their number.—The severe penalty meted out by God made them conscious of how great sincerity and purity of life, and devotion to Christian principles, were required of them.

6. *Divine guidance.*— God kept his people, even by severest judgment, from the corrupting effects of sin springing up within the Christian community itself.—Divine grace was freely bestowed upon Christ's followers to guide and instruct them, and to give them influence over non-believers.

Literature.—Upon this section see the commentaries on Acts, especially those of GLOAG, HACKETT, MEYER, and the CAMBRIDGE BIBLE. Also McGIFFERT, History of Christianity in the Apostolic Age, p. 67 ; WEIZSÄCKER, Apostolic Age of the Christian Church, Vol. I, pp. 52–58 ; NEANDER, Planting and Training of the Christian Church, Vol. I, pp. 24–28 ; STIFLER, Introduction to the Book of Acts, sec. v ; COBB, The Fellowship of Goods in the Apostolic Church (an article in the Presbyterian and Reformed Review, January, 1897).

Sec. 5. APOSTOLIC MIRACLE-WORKING AND FURTHER JEWISH PERSECUTION.

Acts 5 : 12–42.   About 32–33 A. D.   Jerusalem.

I. Study of the Facts.

Let the following subclassification and abstract of the material in this section be verified, corrected, or improved :

Par. 1. 5 : 12–16, Activity and Strength of the Christians.

Par. 2. 5 : 17, 18, Second Imprisonment of the Apostles.

Par. 3. 5 : 19–21a, Miraculous Release and Preaching in the Temple.

Par. 4. 5 : 21b–25, Consultation of the Sanhedrin.

Par. 5. 5 : 26–32, The Arrest, Trial, and Defense of the Apostles.

Par. 6. 5 : 33–39, The Counsel of Gamaliel.

Par. 7. 5 : 40–42, Dismissal of the Apostles after Scourging.

Abstract.— The apostles worked many miracle-signs of healing among the sick in Jerusalem, because of which there was great reverence for the Christians among the people, and many additions to their number. The movement was gaining so much strength and prestige that once more the Sadducees undertook to check it. The apostles were thrown into prison, but the same night were providentially released, and on the next day were again teaching in the temple. A second arrest followed, and a trial before the Sanhedrin, where they were called to account for their disobedience to the previous injunction of that body. They replied that their supreme duty was to preach the message and authority of Christ to men. The Sadducees would have tried violent measures had not Gamaliel, representing the Pharisaic members of the Sanhedrin, intervened with counsels of moderation. A more lenient decision prevailed. The apostles were scourged and dismissed, with the same injunction to cease their teaching of the gospel. As before, they continued their teaching confidently and energetically, for the people were with them.

II. Topics for Investigation.

1. *Apostolic miracle-working.*—Note carefully the information on this subject which is contained in vss. 12–16. Is the expression, "by the hands of" (vs. 12), to be understood literally (*cf.* Josh. 14:2 ; Mark 6:5 ; 16:18)?   Recall also the miracle recorded in Acts 3.   Did all of the apostles work miracles (*cf.* 2:43 ; 5:12)?   Did others than the apostles also work them (*cf.* 6:8 ; 8:6, 7, 13)?   Were they of any other kind than the healing of the sick?   What was the divine purpose in the working of them?   Is it definitely stated that any sick were cured by the shadow of Peter falling upon them, or was that only their super-stitious idea?   Is there any objection to believing that Peter could heal without corporeal contact?   What is to be understood (vs. 15) regarding these shadow cures?   Compare the somewhat similar account of miracles of healing by Paul in Acts 19:11, 12.   Compare the apostolic miracles with Christ's miracles as regards frequency, nature, variety, wonderfulness, and influence.   In whose name did Jesus work miracles (*cf.* John 5:19 ; 11:41 ; Mark 5:41 ; Luke 7:14, and else-where)?   In whose name did the apostles work miracles (*cf.* Acts 3:6 ; 4:10 ; 9:40, and elsewhere)?   What is the significance of the differ-ence ?

2. *Activity and prestige of the Christians.*—Observe that vss. 12–16 form one of the frequent short paragraphs descriptive of the gen-eral condition of the Christian community (*cf.* Acts 2:42, 43–47 ; 4:32–35 ; 12:24, 25, and elsewhere).   The number of Christians is constantly and rapidly growing (vs. 14), "multitudes" being added to the disciples, and the count is no longer kept (*cf.* Acts 1:15 ; 2:41 ; 4:4).   Where was the center of their evangelistic work (*cf.* vss. 12, 20, 21, 25, 42)?   What was the reason of this?   How was this possible since the rulers were so hostile?   What was the attitude of the people toward the Christians, and why?   Explain in detail the meaning of vs. 13.   What success attended the work of the apostles?   Consider the fidelity, energy, and courage of the Christians in their work.   How did God show them that he was protecting and guiding them?   What was the Christian principle on which the apostles could rejoice in their suffering (vs. 41, *cf.* Matt. 5:10–12 ; 10:16–39 ; Acts 16:23–25 ; Rom. 5:3 ; Gal. 6:14 ; 2 Cor. 6:8–10)?   What effect upon them had the punishment and prohibition of the Sanhedrin?   What is meant by "at home" in vs. 42?   What is the difference between the teaching and preaching noted in vs. 42?

3. *The Jewish Sanhedrin.*—When and under what circumstances was the Jewish Sanhedrin instituted? What is the meaning and the origin of the name Sanhedrin? Of how many members was it composed? What different classes or parties were represented in its membership? How were the Sanhedrists appointed? What were the duration, qualifications, and duties of office? Who presided over the body? What was the relative strength of the Sadducees and Pharisees in the Sanhedrin at this apostolic time? Which party led in the opposition to Christ, and why? Which party led in the early opposition to the apostles, and why? What were the functions of the Sanhedrin? How was its power at this time limited? What were the range and scope of its jurisdiction? Where were the sessions of the Sanhedrin held? What was the method of procedure in trials? Consider the relation of the Sanhedrin to John the Baptist, Jesus, Peter, Stephen, Paul. Why was the Sanhedrin the bitterest persecutor of Christianity?

4. *Proceedings and outcome of the second trial.*—Compare this trial carefully in detail with the former trial recorded in Acts 4:1–22. Who were the leaders in that trial, and in this? What charge was brought against the apostles in each? What was the purpose of the miraculous release of the apostles, and what effect, if any, did it have upon the Sanhedrin? State in full the reasons for the jealousy of the Sadduceans against the Christians (vss. 17, 24). What did they admit (vs. 28) as to the success and strength of the Christian movement? How would that "bring this man's blood upon" them (vs. 28)? What defense did the apostles make to the charge of disobedience? Compare this with their defense in the previous trial (4:8–12). How could their disregard of the injunction of the Sanhedrin be justified (*cf.* Rom. 13:1–7; 1 Peter 2:13, 14)? What did the Sadducees wish to do with the apostles? How were violent measures thwarted? What judgment was finally rendered against the apostles? Why were they scourged? Was there any probability that they would cease "to speak in the name of Jesus"? Did they continue as before in their gospel mission? What effect did the trial have upon the progress of the gospel?

5. *The counsel of Gamaliel.*—What was Gamaliel's ancestry? What was his position as a teacher and Sanhedrist (*cf.* Acts 22:3)? What was his personal attitude toward Christianity? Consider carefully the question why Gamaliel counseled moderation toward the Christians.

Was it due to a tolerant spirit?   Was it due to a wisdom gained from historical observation?   Was it due to opposition to the Sadducees, himself being a Pharisee?   Did Gamaliel exert only an individual influence, or did he speak on this occasion as the representative of the Pharisaic element in the Sanhedrin?   Why did the Sadducees accede to Gamaliel's advice?   Was it because they were persuaded that tolerance was better than violence, or because they could not carry their measures against the Pharisaic majority in the Sanhedrin (*cf.* Acts 23:6–9)?   Had they reason also to fear the people, who were supporting the Christians (*cf.* vs. 26)?   Ascertain what further can be known about the two historical incidents cited by Gamaliel.

III. Observations and Teachings.

1. *Organization.*—The apostles were arrested and brought to trial as the leaders of the Christian movement.—The body of Christians was growing constantly and rapidly, so that their number was no longer recorded.

2. *Environment.*—The people regarded the Christians with awe and reverence, and many of them joined the disciples.—The Sadducees were fearful that the Christian movement would sweep everything before it; the city of Jerusalem was filled with their teaching.—This meeting of the Sanhedrin was larger, more formal, and more impassioned than the previous one.

3. *Institutions.*—Does the present section contribute any information on this subject?

4. *Belief and teaching.*—The meaning of Jesus' life, death, and exaltation was plainly preached to the Sanhedrists.—Obedience to God's commands superseded obedience to the commands of any human authorities.—Persecution for the sake of the gospel was gladly borne by the apostles.

5. *Daily life.*—The temple was a general meeting place of the Christians, and was also at this time the center of the public work.—Miracles were worked by the apostles as testimonials to their authority and as a summons of attention to their teaching.—The apostles did not in the least remit their evangelizing activities because of the prohibitory injunctions of the Sanhedrin.

6. *Divine guidance.*—The Christians were given power and grace to attract and win many converts to the gospel, and to create a feeling

of awe and reverence toward their cause.—Miraculous release from imprisonment was given the apostles, as a testimony to their divine mission.

Literature.— Upon this section see the commentaries on Acts, especially those of GLOAG, HACKETT, MEYER, and the CAMBRIDGE BIBLE. Also McGIFFERT, History of Christianity in the Apostolic Age, pp. 74–76, 81–85; NEANDER, Planting and Training of the Christian Church, Vol. I, pp. 46–48; STIFLER, Introduction to the Book of Acts, sec. vi; FARRAR, Life and Work of St. Paul, Bk. I, ch. 6. On the Sanhedrin, see the article upon that subject in the BIBLE DICTIONARY; SEIDEL, In the Time of Jesus, Bk. II, ch. 3; SCHÜRER, Jewish People in the Time of Christ, sec. 23; STAPFER, Palestine in the Time of Christ, Bk. I, ch. 5.

Acts 6: 1–7.   About 32–33 A. D.   Jerusalem.

I. STUDY OF THE FACTS.

Let the following subclassification and abstract of the material in this section be verified, corrected, or improved:

Par. 1. 6:1–6, Appointment of the First Formal Christian Officers.

Par. 2. 6:7, The Christians Increase in Numbers and Strength.

Abstract.—After the persecution by the Sadducees had ceased the work of evangelization went on rapidly, and multitudes of converts joined the Christian movement. But trouble arose between two elements in the Christian community, the Palestinian and the Hellenistic Jews, because in the daily distribution of the charities the needy among the latter class were neglected. A complaint was entered against the neglect or partiality shown. In order to restore justice and harmony the apostles called a full meeting of the disciples. The facts were presented. The trouble had been largely due to the excessive duties of the apostles, who were unable properly to attend to all of them. They therefore asked to be relieved of this portion of their work, so that they might give themselves wholly to teaching and preaching the gospel. They recommended that the body of Christians appoint, from their own number, seven holy and wise men, who should assume the duties of overseeing and dispensing the charitable fund and supplies of the community. This proposal was cordially received. Seven men were at once chosen, Stephen the most prominent of them, and they were commended to the apostles for the approval of their appointment. The apostles ordained them to their work with prayer and the laying on of hands. The internal discord having thus been allayed, the gospel spread widely and grew in strength. Great accessions were all the time being made to the Christian company, and notable among these converts were many Jews of the priest class, who had become convinced of Jesus' Messiahship.

II. TOPICS FOR INVESTIGATION.

1. *The dissension among the Jerusalem Christians.*—When did this trouble arise among the disciples in Jerusalem? Observe the repeated

mention of the growing numbers in the Christian community, Acts 1 : 15; 2 : 41; 4 : 4; 5 : 14; 6 : 1, 7.   Why is the conversion of a large number of the priest class of the Jews especially mentioned ?   Who were the " Grecian Jews" (vs. 1, R. V. mg. "Hellenists")?   Recall the main facts about the Jews of the Dispersion.   How came there to be some of them resident in Jerusalem at this time ?   Is it to be understood that the ones mentioned here belonged to the Christian community ?   Who were the "Hebrews" (vs. 1) as compared with the "Grecian Jews"?   Were these " Hebrews" Christians also ?   When Jews of the Dispersion returned to reside in Jerusalem how were they treated by the Palestinian Jews, and why ?   Had the Hellenistic Jews synagogues of their own in the city, separate from those of the Palestinian Jews (cf. Acts 6 : 9)?   What would be the natural result of bringing together these hostile Jewish factions into one Christian community ?   Why were the Christians at this time not being persecuted ?   Did the truth receive verification that persecution compels unity, while peace permits discord ?   What was the nature of the trouble which now arose ?   Observe that "neglected" (vs. 1) signifies in the Greek repeated or habitual neglect.   Why are " widows" particularly mentioned as the sufferers from this neglect ?   What was the "daily ministration" (vs. 1)?   Was the ground of complaint favoritism or negligence, and on the part of whom ?   How far was the trouble due to the ill-feeling between Palestinian and Hellenistic Jews ?   What was the proportion of each in the Christian community ?   Consider the readiness of the apostles, and of the Christians generally, to remove the cause of this dissension by providing against partiality or neglect.   Describe briefly the steps taken for restoring harmony.   How successful was the new arrangement ?

2. *The new office of alms distributors.*— Explain the meaning of the apostles' statement in vs. 2.   What had been the method up to this time of distributing charity to the needy among the disciples ?   Why had this method become inadequate ?   Why were there so many in the Jerusalem community who were dependent upon this help ?   Who suggested the establishment of this new office ?   What was the new method of alms distribution contemplated in it ?   Was there a set title at this time for this office or these officers ?   Were the duties of the office to some extent similar to those later performed in the churches by the deacons?   Observe that the Greek word translated "ministration" in vs. 1 is *diakonia*, the corresponding agent noun is *diakonos*, from which our word "deacon" is derived.   May this office

now established therefore be considered the precursor of the diaco-
nate ?   On the use of the term "deacon" in the New Testament compare Phil. 1:1 and 1 Tim. 3:8–13.   What qualifications were necessary on the part of these new officers ?   How were they inducted into
office ?   What was the significance of the laying on of hands (cf. Gen.
48:14; Num. 27:18–23; Acts 8:19; 13:3; 19:6; 2 Tim. 1:6)?
Consider that the new office grew simply out of the practical needs of
the Christians.

   3. *The seven men appointed to the office.*— Why was the number of
the alms distributors seven ?   What was the method of election pur-
sued in their appointment, as concerns the parts taken respectively by
the apostles and by the disciples in general ?   Consider carefully the
reasons for the three qualities mentioned by the apostles (vs. 3) as necessary for these new officers.   What was the nationality of these seven
men ?   Were they all Hellenistic Jews with the exception of one
Nicolas, a Gentile who had become a Jewish proselyte and then a
Christian ?   What was the significance of this ?   In this adjustment
of matters so that the Hellenistic Jewish Christians should stand on
equal terms with Palestinian Jewish Christians in the community of
disciples do we see a decided step toward a universal gospel, in
which all nationalities should have equal rights and recognition ?
Can it be said that in this dissension there appeared: (*a*) the line
along which division and bitter strife were to form in the early
church; (*b*) the comprehensive, spiritual character of the gospel
which was to become all embracing ?   Of these seven men made
alms distributors, who are the two which appear in the subsequent
history of Acts, and what about them (cf. Acts 6:8—7:60; 8:4–40;
21:8, 9)?

   4. *The Jewish synagogue and the Christian organization.*— Did
Jesus instruct his disciples as to the form of organization which they
should adopt after his departure ?   Did he even suggest a form ?
Why not ?   Did the disciples set out with a prearranged plan of
organization for the Christian community ?   Had there been as yet a
break between Judaism as such and Christianity, or were the Christians still only a Jewish sect ?   Were the meeting places of the first
Christians called synagogues (cf. James 2:2 R. V.)?   Would it be
natural and appropriate that the Christian church, which assumed a
formal organization only as this became necessary to its life and work,
should adopt the synagogue pattern of organization, adapting it to its
uses ?   Was the new office of alms distributor suggested by some sim-

ilar office in the synagogue ?   When was the office of elder introduced
into the churches (first referred to in Acts 11:30, but probably established some years before)?   Was it perhaps after the dispersion from
Jerusalem (Acts 8), when the Christian communities became so numerous and so widespread that the apostles could not superintend them
all, and individual ruling officers therefore became necessary in each ?
Was there a similar office in the synagogue?   How else, if at all, did
the Christian organization resemble the Jewish synagogue ?

III.   Observations and Teachings.

1.   *Organization.*—The first step was now taken in the development
of a formal Christian organization.—The distribution of goods to the
needy of the Christian community, until now superintended by the
apostles, had become so large a task that special officers were necessary for it.—The new office was perhaps an adaptation of a similar
office in the Jewish synagogue.—The first men appointed to the
office were either all, or in part, Hellenistic Jewish Christians, who
could best correct the injustice which had attended the alms distribution.

2.   *Environment.*—The Grecian Jews (Hellenists) were Jews of the
Dispersion who had grown up in Greek or other foreign communities,
but were now resident in Jerusalem.—The Jews who had never left
Palestine considered that only they were the pure Jewish stock, the
faithful and consistent Jews before Jehovah, so that they looked down
upon and often despised the Jews of the Dispersion.—The Christians
were at this time free from external persecution, the Sadducees having
not accomplished much in their attempts, and the Pharisees still not
being thoroughly aroused.—It was a signal victory for the gospel that
a large number of Jews of the priest class became converted about this
time to a belief in the Messiahship of Jesus ; Christianity was thus
drawing from the high and influential classes of Jews as well as from
the lower classes.

3.   *Institutions.*—The daily ministration to the needy in the Christian community was an important institution among the early Christians.—The neglect of the widows of the Christian Hellenists grew out
of the fact that the apostles had more duties than they could well perform, and the discharge of this particular duty had fallen into preju-
diced or incompetent hands.—The new office of alms distributors was
established by popular vote of all the disciples, upon the recommendation and approval of the apostles, as was also the election of the

first seven men to the office.— Prayer and the laying on of hands were used in the induction of the new officers.

4. *Belief and teaching.*—The new officers must be men of unimpeachable character, filled with the spirit of Christ, and with prudence and experience for the duties which would fall to them.—That form of Christian organization was regarded as the best which was most perfectly adapted to the circumstances in which the Christians were, at a given time or place, called upon to carry on the work of the gospel.

5. *Daily life.*—The number of the Christians continued to grow rapidly from day to day.—This dissension, which arose by reason of discordant elements brought together into a single community, was easily and quickly removed.—The apostles regarded it as their especial duty to teach and preach the gospel.—Stephen was a man already conspicuous and influential among the Christians because of his spiritual faith and power.

6. *Divine guidance.*— During this period of peace the body of disciples grew strong numerically and spiritually, in providential preparation for the murderous persecution which was soon to sweep Stephen away and scatter the Christians from Jerusalem.— When the conditions of the Christian community changed the apostles were divinely led to take such steps as would best provide for the new conditions.

Literature.— Upon this section see the commentaries on Acts, especially those of GLOAG, HACKETT, MEYER, and the CAMBRIDGE BIBLE. Also McGIFFERT, History of Christianity in the Apostolic Age, pp. 76–81 ; WEIZSÄCKER, Apostolic Age of the Christian Church, Vol. I, pp. 43–49 ; RAMSAY, St. Paul the Traveler, pp. 372–377 ; NEANDER, Planting and Training of the Christian Church, Vol. I, pp. 28–40 ; SCHAFF, History of the Christian Church, Vol. I, 455–460, 499–501 ; STIFLER, Introduction to the Book of Acts, sec. vii ; BIBLE DICTIONARY, article Deacon.

SEC. 7. THE PREACHING OF STEPHEN AND ITS CONSE-QUENCES.

Acts 6:8--7:60.   33 A. D.   Jerusalem.

I. STUDY OF THE FACTS.

Let the following subclassification and abstract of the material in this section be verified, corrected, or improved:

Par. 1. 6:8–10,   The Character and Activity of Stephen.
Par. 2. 6:11—7:1, Arraignment of Stephen before the Sanhedrin.
Par. 3. 7:2-53,   Stephen's Defense of his Teaching.

　(1) 2–16, exposition of the Patriarchal history.
　(2) 17–43, exposition of the Mosaic history.
　(3) 44–50, exposition of the Royal and Prophetic history.
　(4) 51–53, denunciation of the present generation of Jews.

Par. 4. 7:54-60,   The Condemnation and Death of Stephen.

Abstract.—The spiritual grace, power, and activity of Stephen made him one of the greatest of the Christian leaders in these first years. Being himself a Hellenist, he especially worked among the Hellenistic Jews in Jerusalem, urging Christianity upon them and arguing in defense of Christ in their synagogues. He taught that Judaism was superseded by the gospel, that Jesus had done away (or at his second coming would do away) with the temple and all cere-monialism, so that religion should henceforth be a wholly spiritual matter. This view was based upon Jesus' own teaching, but the dis-ciples had been constrained by their love for Judaism to neglect this practical bearing of their Master's words. Stephen's teaching could not but arouse the most violent hatred and opposition of the Pharisees and Jews generally, such as Christ himself had experienced. He was brought to trial before the Sanhedrin on the charge of blasphemy against the most sacred institutions of Judaism. In his defense Stephen with apologetic aim reviewed briefly the history of the Hebrew people, and drew therefrom an argument for the freedom and spirit-uality of religion, particularly in connection with the temple of Sol-omon. Their impatience broke out in threats and interruption apparently, for Stephen left the historical argument he had been developing, and in a few words of utmost severity he rebuked them for their resistance to spiritual truth and revelation.   This enraged the Sanhedrists beyond measure, and without staying for a formal con- demnation they hurried him out of the city and stoned him to death, as the law required for the blasphemer.   With perfect Christian forti- tude and forgiveness Stephen received his martyrdom, as Jesus before him had done.

II.   TOPICS FOR INVESTIGATION.

1. *Stephen.*— Is Acts 6 : 1–7 introductory to this further account of Stephen ?   How long a time should be supposed to intervene between vs. 7 and vs. 8 ?   Consider whether Stephen is in vs. 8 represented as a miracle-worker, and if so whether he is the first such recorded in New Testament history who was not one of the Twelve.   What official position did Stephen occupy among the Christians ?   Recall the occa- sion of his election to that office.   What were the chief characteristics of Stephen ?   Was he a Hellenistic Jew ?   Would this probable fact bear any relation to the large conception of the gospel which he preached ?   Did he belong to one of the five Hellenistic synagogues in Jerusalem mentioned in vs. 9 ?   Can we tell which one ?   Locate upon the map the different countries there mentioned.   Why did the Jews from these various places have separate synagogues in Jerusalem ? Was it because Stephen was called to account by them for his Christian belief and activity that he "disputed" (vs. 9) with them, or because he undertook to evangelize his Hellenist friends ?   What were Stephen's character and power in this presentation and defense of Christianity ? Why did his opponents resort to violent methods for suppressing him ?

2. *The teaching of Stephen.*— Define as exactly as possible what Stephen's conception and teaching of the gospel was, which aroused the Jewish opposition.   How did it differ from the view of the gos- pel held and taught by the Twelve ?   How is the difference of view to be accounted for ?   Whence did Stephen derive his doctrine ?   Did Stephen or the Twelve best represent Jesus' teaching on the subject involved ?   Was the main point in Stephen's conception the abolition of Jewish ritualism, the spiritualization of religious life and worship ? In what sense can Stephen be called the forerunner of Paul ?   Did Stephen's teaching concern primarily the Jews or the Gentiles ?   Had the problem yet been taken up by the primitive Christians whether or not the Gentiles should be *directly* admitted to Christianity ?   To what extent did the Christians support Stephen in his teaching ?

3. *The trial before the Sanhedrin.*—Who instituted the proceedings against Stephen? Why was it necessary to obtain *false* witnesses? What charge was entered against him (vss. 11, 13, 14; *cf.* Deut. 13:6–11)? In what respects was this charge true, and in what respects false? Why were the Pharisees and Jewish people as a whole aroused to hostility in this case? Recall the previous two persecutions of the Christians (Acts 4 and 5), when the Sadducees were the chief persecutors. Explain the charge in this third persecution. What was the method of procedure in this trial? Make a careful comparison of this trial of Stephen with the trial of Jesus.

4. *Stephen's defense.*—What did he undertake to accomplish by his speech before the Sanhedrin? Describe the method which he employed to this end. Would any other line of argument than the historical have served him so well? Consider carefully Stephen's brief review of Hebrew history. With the aid of a marginal reference Bible, make a comparison of the history as recounted by Stephen in chap. 7, with the Old Testament records. Explain the apparent discrepancies in the history in vss. 2b–4a, 4b, 5a, 6d, 16a, 16b. Name the chief characteristics of this speech of Stephen in defense of his teaching. Was the speech interrupted at vs. 51 by the dissent of his hearers? Why should they dissent at this point? Was the argument cut short by their interruption? Consider the terrible severity of Stephen's closing words to the Sanhedrin. Why did the Acts historian give this extended account of Stephen's speech? How was it preserved for transmission in Acts?

5. *The martyrdom of Stephen.*—Did the trial end with a formal condemnation of Stephen by the Sanhedrin, or did it break up in a furious onslaught upon him? Was the Sanhedrin so far responsible for the death of Stephen that it may be looked upon as a legal execution, or was it a murder? Explain how the former might take place, even though the Sanhedrin had not properly the right of capital punishment. Why was stoning the means used to put Stephen to death (*cf.* Lev. 24:16)? What was the method of procedure in a legal execution by stoning? Was this procedure followed in this case? Consider the character of Stephen as disclosed in his martyrdom. Compare his manner of meeting death with that of Jesus. Explain the fact that Stephen is reported as using the title "Son of Man" (vs. 56), the only instance in the New Testament outside of the gospels where this title is used of Jesus, though it was the special title which he chose for himself. Why is the fact mentioned that Paul (Saul) was

present at the martyrdom of Stephen? Had he any part in his death? Consider and explain in this connection Acts 22 : 20; also Acts 8 : 1. Had this relation of Paul with Stephen any influence upon Paul's conversion to Christianity some months later?

III. OBSERVATIONS AND TEACHINGS.

1. *Organization.*— Does the present section contribute any information on this subject?

2. *Environment.*— This third conflict of the Christians with the Sanhedrin was much more severe than the former two, because the Pharisees were the chief persecutors.— For the first time the common people joined in the opposition, believing that Christianity was going to destroy the most sacred Jewish institutions.— The Sanhedrists, without a formal condemnation, and attended by an infuriated Jewish mob, stoned Stephen to death.— The Hellenistic Jews had synagogues of their own in Jerusalem, and to one of these Stephen seems to have belonged; there he advanced and defended his new conception of gospel truth.

3. *Institutions.*— Does the present section contribute any information on this subject?

4. *Belief and teaching.*— Stephen, the Hellenist, by reason of his broader view and more open heart, as well as because of his deeper spiritual insight, saw the truth of Christianity more perfectly than any other disciple of his time; he perceived that the religion of Christ was essentially spiritual, and that it was therefore superior to, and must in its full acceptance free itself from, the whole ritualistic and legalistic system of Judaism.— From the Jewish point of view this could be nothing less than blasphemy against God and Moses.— It was the same teaching which brought Jesus to death at their hands.

5. *Daily life.*— Stephen's attitude before the Sanhedrin was one of calm and inspired confidence, a joyful, holy consciousness that he was the ambassador of Christ.— The saintly character of Stephen and his inspired mission were manifest in the glorious manner of his death. — Paul appears to have been one of the interested participants in the persecution and murder of Stephen.

6. *Divine guidance.*— God permits it to be true that the developed stages, enlarged views, and loftier conceptions of religious truth are commonly established only in the face of sincere, violent opposition. — God called Stephen to a martyr's death that the truth of the gospel

might be established through him.— It resulted, by divine providence, that the persecution which Stephen stirred up led to the immediate and wide spread of the gospel throughout Palestine, and even into Syria and elsewhere.

Literature.— Upon this section see the commentaries on Acts, especially those of GLOAG, HACKETT, MEYER, and the CAMBRIDGE BIBLE. Also McGIFFERT, History of Christianity in the Apostolic Age, pp. 85–92; WEIZSÄCKER, Apostolic Age of the Christian Church, Vol. I, pp. 62–72; NEANDER, Planting and Training of the Christian Church, Vol. I, pp. 48–56; Vol. II, pp. 73–79; FARRAR, Life and Work of St. Paul, chap. 7; CONYBEARE AND HOWSON, Life and Epistles of St. Paul, chap. 2; STIFLER, Introduction to the Book of Acts, sec. viii; BIBLE DICTIONARY, article Stephen.

SECOND DIVISION.

PERIOD OF GOSPEL EXPANSION.

Text : Acts 8 : 1—15 : 35.   Time : Seventeen years, 34-50 A. D.   Localities : Palestine, Syria, Galatia.   Leaders : Peter, James, and Paul.

During the first few years of the church the thousands of converts who joined the original body of Christians in Jerusalem were Jews either by descent or by adoption.   But the preaching of Stephen brought on a fierce persecution of the Christians, in consequence of which they were dispersed throughout Palestine and Syria.   Everywhere they at once began to evangelize the communities into which they came.   By this means it was no long time until all classes, both of Jews and of Gentiles, were seeking admission to the Christian churches. Naturally the question arose : must the Gentiles become Jews (*i. e.*, conform to the Jewish ritual, particularly the rite of circumcision) before they could become Christians ; or, in other words, was Christianity the supplemental tenet of a Jewish sect, or was it a universal, spiritual religion for all men and all time ?   The latter was the conception of the gospel as Christ presented it, but much courage, wisdom, and strength were needed to effect its realization.   The pressure toward this catholicity came upon the church through three distinct avenues of experience, as presented in the Book of Acts : (1) Peter's divine vision by which he was led to receive Cornelius and his family who were pure Gentiles, as such into the Christian church ; (2) the efforts of the gospel missionaries in Antioch, where the same policy of Gentile admission was adopted ; (3) Paul's first evangelizing tour in Galatia, where he found it his Christian duty to admit the Gentiles to Christianity on the same plane with the Jews.   In view of these practical experiences, therefore, the gospel idea underwent a rapid and significant expansion during these seventeen years.   Antioch became the Gentile mother-church, and represented the universal conception of Christianity.   The mother-church at Jerusalem was still Jewish in composition and temper, but it had recognized the divine leading of Peter in the case of Cornelius, and was disposed toward an official consideration of the question.   The leaders of the church therefore met in Jerusalem, treated the problem in a general conference, and

39

formally recognized the gospel to be a universal religion to which the
Gentiles had an equal right with the Jews.   The characteristics of this
second period were, then, the extension of the Christian church
through Palestine, Syria, and Galatia; the preparation of men, such
as Paul and Barnabas, who were fit to lead in this work; and the agi-
tation, discussion, and theoretic settlement of this Gentile problem,
which determined the scope of Christianity.   But time was required
for putting this doctrine into effect, and for making the adjustments
necessary in view of it, particularly with regard to the mutual relations
of Gentile and Jewish Christians to each other.   This was to be the
problem and the achievement of the next, the third, period of the
primitive era of Christianity.

Sec. 8. FIRST EXTENSION OF ORGANIZED CHRISTIANITY BEYOND JERUSALEM.

Acts 8 : 1–40.   34 A. D.   Samaria and elsewhere.

I. STUDY OF THE FACTS.

Let the following subclassification of the material in this section be verified, corrected, or improved:

Par. 1. 8 : 1–3,   Violent Persecution and General Dispersion of the Christians.

Par. 2. 8 : 4–8,   The Evangelizing Work of Philip in Samaria.

Par. 3. 8 : 9–13,   The Conversion of Simon the Magian.

Par. 4. 8 : 14–25, The Visit of the Apostolic Deputation to Samaria.

Par. 5. 8 : 26–40, The Conversion of the Ethiopian Treasurer.

Sufficient illustration has been given (in the sections of Division I) of the *Abstract* of the Acts material. The student will now advance from the mere correction of an abstract already prepared to the more difficult work of himself preparing the abstract. Special attention must be directed to the avoidance of the language of the English version. The thoughts and facts of the section should be entirely divorced from the forms of expression in which they are clothed, and then told over again in the student's own language and style. After the abstract is prepared, let it be subjected to the same process of verification, correction, or improvement which has been applied to the printed abstracts.

II. TOPICS FOR INVESTIGATION.

1. *The great persecution and dispersion.* — Review the facts (Acts chaps. 4 and 5) concerning the former two persecutions of the disciples, as to their causes, circumstances, leaders, outcome of the trials, and final results of the persecutions. Explain why in this third persecution, in contrast with the former ones, the Pharisees take the lead and the common people join in the hostility toward the Christians. Recall how Stephen was the one who brought on this persecution. Why did the Christians leave Jerusalem? What proportion of them went away? Is there anything in the records to indicate that there was a Stephen party among the Christians, that they rather than all the Christians were the objects of the persecution, and that only they were

compelled to leave the city?   Or was the persecution indiscriminate,
affecting all Christians alike?   How could the apostles remain in Jerusalem, considering that they were the conspicuous heads of the offend-
ing company and had before this time been singled out for trial and
punishment?   Whither did the Christians go from Jerusalem?   Was
their departure from the city permanent, or did they return when the
persecution waned?   What was Paul's relation to the death of Stephen
(cf. Acts 7 : 58; 8 : 1; 22 : 20)?   Exactly what is meant by "gave my
vote against them" (Acts 26 : 10)?   Consider Paul's own descriptions
of his persecution of the Christians, Acts 22 : 4, 19, 20; 26 : 9–11; Gal.
1 : 13, 23; I Cor. 15 : 9.   Why was Paul so uncompromisingly hostile to
Christianity?   How did he justify his action (cf. Deut. 13 : 6–10; 17 :
2–7; Lev. 24 : 10–16)?   What was the good providentially flowing
from this persecution and dispersion?

2. *Samaria and the Samaritans.*— Locate Samaria upon the map.
Ascertain something as to the history of the Samaritans (cf. 2 Kings
17 : 1–41; Ezra 4 : 1–24; Josephus' *Antiq.* 10. 9. 7; 9. 14. 3).   How
largely Jewish were the Samaritans in the first century A. D.?   What
was the attitude of the Judean Jews toward them (cf. John 4 : 9; 8 : 48;
Josephus' *Antiq.* 20. 6. 1; 9. 14. 3)?   What was the difference between
the Samaritans and the Judean Jews as regarded the Old Testament
Scriptures?   What were the peculiarities of the Samaritan religious
belief and practice?   Were they better prepared to receive the gospel
than the strict Jews?   If so, why?   Consider the work done by Jesus and
his disciples in Samaria (cf. John 4 : 1–42; Luke 9 : 51–56; 17 : 11–19;
and elsewhere).   Would some of the dispersed Christians settle, at least
temporarily, in Samaria?

3. *Philip and his work in Samaria.*— Is this Philip one of the Seven
of Acts 6 : 5?   Why did he take up evangelizing work in Samaria?
What was Philip's message to the Samaritans (cf. Acts 8 : 5, 12)?   Why
has there been no mention before this in Acts of the preaching of the
"kingdom of God" (Jesus' one great theme)?   How was the truth of
Philip's message attested (cf. Acts 8 : 6, 7, 13)?   What was the success
of Philip's work?   State and briefly describe the business of Simon the
Magian?   Why did magianism have so strong a hold upon the people
at this time?   What influence had Simon in Samaria?   Was he an
impostor, or an honest worker in the mysteries of nature?   Why did the
gospel appeal to him?   Why did he make the strange request for which
Peter rebuked him?   May we regard Simon as having become a true
Christian?   Do we hear anything further of the Samaritan Christians?

4. *The apostolic deputation.*—What especial interest and significance would the report of Philip's success in Samaria have for the
apostles at Jerusalem?   What was the purpose of the apostles in sending representatives thither : (*a*) because through the Jewish distrust of
the Samaritans, the report was doubted; (*b*) lack of confidence in
Philip's ability to do the work well; (*c*) jealousy of the success which
the Hellenist Philip was having; (*d*) to extend fellowship to the new
converts, and affiliate them with the Jerusalem Christians ; (*e*) to bestow
the special gifts of the Spirit.   Why were Peter and John chosen for
this mission?   What did they do when they arrived?   What was the
character of the baptism which the Samaritan converts received from
Philip?   What was the need of a further baptism by the apostles?   Was
the presence and work of the apostles essential to the founding of this
Christian community in Samaria?   Did the action of Peter and John
affiliate the Samaritan with the Judean Christians?   Consider this
evangelizing of Samaria as an additional step toward the universal gospel, inasmuch as the Samaritans were, and especially were regarded as,
a mixed race, partly Gentile.

5. *Philip and the Ethiopian treasurer.*—Trace on the map the road
(vs. 26) between Jerusalem and Gaza.   Indicate on the map the location of Ethiopia, and ascertain something about the inhabitants and the
history of that country.   Why had this treasurer of the queen of Ethiopia been to Jerusalem?   Of what nationality was he—a Gentile or a
Jew?   If the former, was he a Jewish proselyte?   Why was he interested at this time in Messianic prophecy?   Had he learned in Jerusalem something about Jesus and his Messianic claims?   Consider the
providence which brought Philip to the man in his search for the truth.
What is the Messianic teaching of Isa. 53 : 7–9, which needed explanation to the Ethiopian treasurer?   How would Philip present Jesus to
him?   What was the result of Philip's conference with him?   Explain
the omission of vs. 37 from the Revised Version.   Why has this incident received so full a report in the Acts history?   How was it connected with the development of the universal gospel?   Have we yet
reached the stage of development at which Gentiles were admitted to
Christianity without entering through the gateway of Judaism?

III.   OBSERVATIONS AND TEACHINGS.

Reconsider carefully the directions regarding this part of the study given at this point in Section 1.

1. *Organization* —According to the Acts account the apostles
remained at Jerusalem through the persecution and dispersion, keep-

ing up communication with the scattered Christians, and maintaining authority over their evangelizing activities.—A deputation was sent by them to inspect the work done by Philip in Samaria, to approve and affiliate the new converts, and to communicate to them the peculiar blessings and power of the Holy Spirit.

2. *Environment.*—A crisis in the life of the Christian community at Jerusalem was brought about by the combined and violent hostility of the Jewish religious leaders and their popular following.—The Christians were persecuted so severely that large numbers of them left the city, for at least a time.—Paul rose to prominence as a leader among the persecutors, thus early in the history of the primitive church becoming one of the chief figures.

3. *Institutions.*—The laying on of hands was used by the apostles in appointing men to office (6:6) and in the Holy Spirit baptism (8:17) as a symbol of the impartation of needed gifts and graces.

4. *Belief and teaching.*—By the apostolic recognition and adoption to fellowship of the Samaritan Christians, another long and significant step was taken toward a universal gospel.—The Ethiopian treasurer, who was presumably either a devout Jew or a Jewish proselyte, was divinely led into a knowledge of the truth concerning Christ through Philip.

5. *Daily life.*—The dispersed Christians engaged at once, everywhere in Palestine and even in more distant places, in preaching the gospel.—Philip became one of the most earnest and successful workers in this great missionary movement.—Among Philip's converts in Samaria was one Simon, a magian, who did not at first free himself wholly from business considerations in connection with the new profession of the gospel.—Philip made an evangelizing tour northward along the west coast of Palestine until he reached Cæsarea.

6. *Divine guidance.*—During the few years between Christ's death and this dispersion the Christian community in Jerusalem had assumed a stable and definite character; the scattering of the Christians which now took place providentially resulted in the spread of organized Christianity throughout Palestine, and even in Syria and other distant countries.—The faithful study of the Scriptures is one of God's broad avenues into a knowledge of his truth and of his Messiah.

Literature.— Upon this section see the commentaries on Acts, especially those of GLOAG, HACKETT, MEYER, and the CAMBRIDGE BIBLE. Also McGIFFERT, History of Christianity in the Apostolic Age, pp. 92-101; NEANDER, Planting and Training of the Christian Church, Vol. I, pp. 57-66; CONYBEARE AND HOWSON, Life and Epistles of St. Paul, chap. 3; STIFLER, Introduction to the Book of Acts, sec. viii; BIBLE DICTIONARY, articles Ethiopia, Philip, Samaria, Simon (Magus), Sorcerer.

SEC. 9. THE CONVERSION OF PAUL FROM JUDAISM TO CHRISTIANITY.

Acts 9 : 1–19a; *cf.* 22 : 6–16 and 26 : 13–18.   34 A. D.   Damascus.

I. STUDY OF THE FACTS.

Let the following subclassification of the material in this section be verified, corrected, or improved :

Par. 1. 9 : 1, 2,   Persecution of the Damascus Christians.
Par. 2. 9 : 3–9,   The Revelation of Jesus to Paul.
Par. 3. 9 : 10–19a, The Divine Commission through Ananias.

1. Prepare an abstract, in your own language, of the facts recorded in this section. Make it as well proportioned and as accurate as possible.

2. Of the incidents attending the conversion of Paul there are three distinct narratives: (1) Acts 9 : 3–19a ; (2) Acts 22 : 6–16 ; (3) Acts 26 : 12–18. To arrive at the exact facts, therefore, it is necessary to make a careful comparative study of all three accounts. This the student is expected to do, working out of all three the harmonized details of the events. Let the most important differences in the three narratives be noted and explained, and a decision be reached as to which account is most trustworthy.

II. TOPICS FOR INVESTIGATION.

1. *Paul's mission to Damascus.*— What is the connection between Acts 9 : 1 and 8 : 1–3 ? Observe the titles used in this chapter to designate the Christians : "disciples" (vs. 1), those "of the way" (vs. 2), and "saints" (vs. 13) ; with the aid of a concordance look up other passages where these designations occur. Locate Damascus upon the map, and learn something about the city as it then was. How came there to be Christians in that city ? Why was this persecution of the disciples carried as far as Damascus ? Why did Paul secure letters from the high priest for this mission ? What was the purport of them ? What did the Sanhedrin at Jerusalem have to do with the synagogues in Damascus or elsewhere ? Explain how the disciples were subject to legal persecution for their adherence to Christ. What was to be done with Christians found in Damascus ?

2. *The revelation of Jesus to Paul.*—Observe and consider separately the incidents connected with the vision : *a*) vicinity of Damascus, *b*) midday, *c*) shekinah, *d*) in which Jesus appeared to Paul, *e*) stunning blindness, *f*) a voice from heaven, *g*) Jesus' question, "Saul, Saul," etc., *h*) Jesus' word, "It is hard," etc., *i*) Paul's reply, "Who art thou, Lord?" *j*) Jesus' answer, "I am," etc., *k*) Paul's second question, "What wilt," etc., *l*) command to go into the city and receive his commission, *m*) continued blindness, *n*) three days' fast. Why should the revelation to Paul have been attended by such striking circumstances? What was the need of the vision itself to Paul? Why did it come just at that time? Explain Jesus' words to Paul, "It is hard for thee to kick against the goad" (omitted by R. V. from 9 : 5; *cf.* 26 : 14). What did Paul mean by his question, "Who art thou, Lord?" What was the providential purpose of the blindness which came upon Paul? Why the long fast and waiting before he received his commission? What were Paul's spiritual experiences during this period? Consider whether Paul's vision of Jesus was internal or external, subjective or objective, physical or spiritual. Would either kind of vision have accomplished the purpose of the revelation? Compare Paul's vision of Jesus at this time with Jesus' resurrection appearances to the Twelve; were they parallel, and with similar aim?

3. *Paul's preparation for this crisis.*—Consider whether Paul had been providentially prepared for receiving this revelation of Jesus, *a*) by his natural temperament — humane, sincere, and loyal to religious truth; *b*) by his birth and education — a Hellenistic Jew, trained in the liberal school of Gamaliel, and associated with Hellenists; *c*) by his contact with Christian truth — in the Christian preaching, especially of Stephen, which, as a deep thinker and a mentally trained man, he would profoundly consider; *d*) by his contact with the Christians themselves— witnessing their fine courage, joy, forgiveness, faith, traits nobler than his own religion produced; *e*) by his own spiritual unrest—he had kept the law blamelessly but was not at peace (*cf.* Rom. 7); *f*) by his present inhuman inquisition — his religion had led him into brutal bloodshed and persecution, which he realized was ungodlike and wrong. He was therefore searching for the new light, especially as he meditated upon his course while he journeyed to Damascus.

4. *The conversion of Paul.*— What was Paul's moral and religious character previous to his vision of Jesus (*cf.* Phil. 3 : 6; Acts 23 : 1; 1 Tim. 1 : 13; Acts 26 : 9; Gal. 1 : 14; also John 16 : 2, 3)? Was he completely devoted to the religion of his fathers? Did he earnestly

strive to attain perfection of character by obedience to the law ? Was
he living up to the best religious light of his time before Christ came ?
Why had not Paul become a Christian before this time? Consider
two meanings for the word "conversion :" *a*) a turning from sin to
holiness, a change from wrong purpose to right purpose, a reversal of
moral choice; *b*) a change of ideas, a reversal of belief (and conduct
incident thereto) consequent upon the gaining of new knowledge. In
which of these two senses can we use the term "conversion" to designate this experience of Paul ? Why had he lacked before this the
evidence which would convince him of the Messiahship of Jesus ? Did
the gospel come to him as a divine relief from mistaken thoughts and
mistaken deeds ? Was Paul slower in accepting Jesus and his teaching than were Jesus' immediate followers ?

5. *The divine commission.*— Compare the three different accounts
of the substance and the giving of this commission (*cf.* 9 : 15–17 ;
22 : 14, 15 ; 26 : 16–18). Note and explain the important variations.
Was the commission announced to him by Ananias ? If so, why was
it announced in this way ? Consider the divine communications to
both Paul and Ananias, in preparation for their meeting (*cf.* Acts
10 : 1–23). Was he by Ananias received into Christian brotherhood ?
Consider that the Holy Spirit baptism was administered to Paul by a
common disciple rather than by one of the apostles (*cf.* Acts 8 : 14–
17). Why was Paul called and commissioned apart from the Twelve
(*cf.* Gal. 1 : 16, 17) ? Was Paul's commission at the outset a distinct and
exclusive appointment to the evangelization of the Gentiles, or did it
only later come to be that by force of circumstances (*cf.* Acts 9 : 22–
25 ; 22 : 17–21 ; Gal. 1 : 16 ; Rom. 11 : 13 ; Eph. 3 : 8 ; Rom. 15 : 16 ;
Gal. 2 : 2, 7–9 ; 1 Tim. 2 : 7 ; 2 Tim. 1 : 11) ? How long after Paul's
conversion before he began his work among the Gentiles ? What
peculiar qualifications had Paul for the Gentile mission ? Why had
no one of the original apostles taken up this work ?

III. Observations and Teachings.

1. *Organization.*— Does the present section contribute any information on this subject ?

2. *Environment.*— The persecution of the disciples was carried
even to Damascus, where there seem to have been not a few of them.
—Damascus was the gateway to the East, through which Christianity
might pass to the Jews of the Dispersion in that region ; hence Paul's
mission to that city.— The Pharisee Paul, one of the ablest and most

energetic opponents of Christianity, changed over to the Christian cause.

3. *Institutions.*— Paul received the spirit baptism at Ananias' hands, without the customary mediation of the apostles.

4. *Belief and teaching.*— Paul had had small opportunity to judge of the truth of Jesus' claims or his message ; he lacked evidence to convince him of Jesus' Messiahship.—This evidence was providentially supplied to him by his vision of Jesus.— He immediately accepted the new light and entered upon the mission of giving it to others.— His conversion was not a change of heart and purpose, but of belief and action.

5. *Daily life.*—The revelation was attended by many striking circumstances which would impress Paul and his companions with its supernaturalness and significance.— In many natural and providential ways Paul had been prepared for the revelation of Jesus now given to him.— The agency of Ananias served to affiliate Paul with the Damascus Christians.

6. *Divine guidance.*— Paul was a chosen servant of God for the spread of the gospel, especially among the Gentiles.—The conversion of Paul was a most important step in the development of the universal and spiritual conception of the gospel.

Literature.— Upon this section see the commentaries on Acts, especially those of GLOAG, HACKETT, MEYER, and the CAMBRIDGE BIBLE. Also McGIFFERT, History of Christianity in the Apostolic Age, pp. 113–150 ; WEIZSÄCKER, Apostolic Age of the Christian Church, Vol. I, pp. 79–93 ; NEANDER, Planting and Training of the Christian Church, Vol. I, pp. 77–90 ; Vol. II, pp. 88–94 ; FARRAR, Life and Work of St. Paul, chs. 9 and 10 ; CONYBEARE AND HOWSON, Life and Epistles of St. Paul, ch. 3 ; HATCH, Encyclopædia Britannica, 9th ed., article Paul ; BIBLE DICTIONARY, article Paul ; SCHAFF, History of the Christian Church, Vol. I, pp. 281–316 ; STEVENS, The Pauline Theology, pp. 1–26 ; BRUCE, St. Paul's Conception of Christianity, pp. 26–47 ; MATHESON, Spiritual Development of St. Paul, pp. 45–92 ; SABATIER, The Apostle Paul, pp. 47–67 ; STALKER, Life of St. Paul. ch. 2.

Acts 9 : 19b–31; *cf.* Gal. 1 : 17, 18 (19–24).   34–37 (37–43) A. D.

Damascus, Arabia, Jerusalem, Cilicia.

I. STUDY OF THE FACTS.

Let the following subclassification of the material in this section be verified, corrected, or improved:

Par. 1. 9 : 19b–22, Paul Preaches Jesus as Messiah at Damascus.
Par. 2. 9 : 23–25, His Forced Departure from the City.
Par. 3. 9 : 26–30, Paul's First Visit as a Christian to Jerusalem.
Par. 4. 9 : 31,   Peace and Growth of the Christians.

1. Prepare an abstract of the material contained in this section, giving special attention to accuracy, and originality of language.

2. Observe Paul's own statements in Gal. 1 : 17, 18, concerning the events recorded in Acts at this point, gathering the additional facts given.

II. TOPICS FOR INVESTIGATION.

1. *Three years of work in Damascus.*—How came Paul to be in Damascus? How long after his conversion before he began preaching Christianity? In what places and to whom did Paul preach? What was his message (*cf.* vss. 20, 22)? How would he prove to Jews that Jesus was the Messiah? In view of his divine commission (*cf.* Sec. 9, Topic 5) why did he not preach to the Gentiles instead of to Jews? How long a time did Paul work in Damascus (*cf.* Gal. 1 : 17, 18)? Why does the Acts make no reference to the Arabian sojourn recorded in Gal. 1 : 17? At what point does the sojourn come in the Acts account —between vss. 19a and 19b, or between vss. 22 and 23? Consider the two views of this sojourn : *a)* that it was to Mt. Sinai, extending over a year or more of time, and was given to retirement and meditation ; *b)* that it did not take Paul far from Damascus, that it was of short duration, and that it was probably for escape from immediate danger to himself from his former associates on account of his joining the Christian cause (*cf.* Acts 9 : 29, and the discussions of Ramsay and Weizsäcker cited below). What success attended Paul's work in Damascus? How was it interrupted? What indications does Acts

give as to the length of Paul's stay in Damascus (*cf.* vss. 19 and 23)? Why is this matter left so very indefinite by the historian? On his escape from the city (vs. 25) compare 2 Cor. 11 : 32, 33 (also Josh. 2 : 15; 1 Sam. 19 : 12).

2. *Paul's first Christian visit to Jerusalem.*—How long had Paul been away from the city (*cf.* Acts 9 : 1, 2; Gal. 1 : 18)? Why had he then left the city, and what had happened to his plans? For what purpose was he now returning to Jerusalem (*cf.* Gal. 1 : 18)? What did he wish to accomplish by this acquaintance with Peter : *a)* to establish friendly relations with him in spreading the gospel, *b)* to learn more about the facts of Christ's life and his detailed teachings? How was he received at Jerusalem, and why? Who intervened to set things right? How came Barnabas to know of, and vouch for, Paul's sincerity as a Christian? Whom of the apostles did Paul meet at Jerusalem (*cf.* Gal. 1 : 19), and why not the others also? What did he obtain from this conference? How long did he stay in Jerusalem (*cf.* Gal. 1 : 18)? Does Acts 9 : 28, 29 harmonize with the Galatians representation (1 : 18, 22–24), that Paul went to Jerusalem to visit Peter, stayed but fifteen days, "and was unknown by face to the churches of Judea"? To what class of Jews in Jerusalem did Paul undertake to preach the gospel? Why to them? Compare his experience in this respect with Stephen's (Acts 6 : 9, 10). What attitude did they take toward him, and why? How did he escape from them? With this explanation of his withdrawal from Jerusalem compare the one given by himself in Acts 22 : 17–21, to the effect that he received a directly communicated command from Christ and an immediate commission to the Gentile work. Can the two explanations be adjusted to one another?

3. *Paul's evangelizing activity in Syria and Cilicia.*—Indicate upon the map the route which Paul took in returning to Tarsus, his home. When do we next hear of him (*cf.* Acts 11 : 25, 26)? Where was Paul between his departure from Jerusalem in 37 A. D. and his call to Antioch in 43 A. D. (*cf.* Acts 9 : 30; Gal. 1 : 21)? Was he engaged during this period in preaching the gospel and establishing churches in Syria and Cilicia (*cf.* Acts 15 : 23, 41)? Was Paul in these years addressing himself to Jews chiefly, or to Gentiles—that is, had he yet entered upon his distinctively Gentile mission? In what particulars was this period one of preparation for his subsequent career? Why has so little been recorded about this important period of Paul's work? Consider that Syria and Cilicia formed the next territorial stage in the expansion of the gospel from Jerusalem to Rome.

4. *Condition of the Christians, 37–43 A. D.*— Explain the logical force and connection of the word "so" introducing Acts 9 : 31. Does it mean that Paul's departure from Jerusalem was the cause of the peace which the verse records; or that peace came because of Paul's conversion to Christianity? Ascertain the political situation of these years, as to whether the attention of the Jews was directed away from the Christians to their Roman rulers in the disorders of the reign of Caligula and the early years of Claudius. Consider separately and carefully the three descriptive phrases used concerning the condition of the Christians: "being edified," "walking in the fear of the Lord," and "walking in the comfort of the Holy Ghost." Was it not only a period of rest, but also of growth in strength and numbers? Indicate upon the map the districts where Christianity existed at this time, and endeavor to associate with each district the time when the gospel came to it, the persons especially instrumental in establishing it there, and the character of the belief and the life of the Christians in each district. Where were the twelve apostles during this period? Were the local bodies of Christians organized; if so, in what way? Observe in this verse the term "church" used in a collective sense to denote all of the separate communities of the Christians taken as a whole; as a matter of historical fact, was the term yet used in this sense at this time, or is it a term which came into use later, and was then employed in speaking of the earlier time?

III. Observations and Teachings.

1. *Organization.*— Does the present section contribute any information upon this subject?

2. *Environment.*— Paul began immediately after his conversion an active, earnest preaching of Jesus as Messiah, to the Hellenistic Jews in Damascus, and later he attempted the same in Jerusalem.— Three years after his conversion he went to Jerusalem to visit Peter, intending thus to establish good relations with the original apostles in his preaching of the gospel, and to learn more of Jesus' life and teaching. — As far as the Acts account goes, there was as yet no presentation of the gospel directly to the Gentiles, independently of Judaism; even Paul was working exclusively among Jews.— The presence of severe political trouble, and the conversion of Paul the chief persecutor, caused the Jews for some years to remit their hostility to the Christians.— There were now Christians everywhere in Palestine, and the movement prospered greatly during this period of peace.

3. *Institutions.*— Does the present section contribute any information upon this subject ?

4. *Belief and teaching.*— Paul's intellectual ability, his thorough education and training, his broad and deep knowledge of the Old Testament, and his spiritual experience of Jesus, all combined to make him a most efficient preacher of the gospel.

5. *Daily life.*— The Christians everywhere were increasing in faith and piety, living worthily of their profession, and rejoicing in the gospel.

6. *Divine guidance.*— Paul became at once, upon his conversion, one of the most prominent advocates of Christianity.— Yet, contrary to what might have been supposed, it was God's plan that he should preach the gospel to Gentiles rather than to Jews, and his early years of Christian activity were spent in Syria and Cilicia.

Literature.—Upon this section see the commentaries on Acts, especially those of GLOAG, HACKETT, MEYER, and the CAMBRIDGE BIBLE. Also McGIFFERT, History of Christianity in the Apostolic Age, pp. 161–172 ; WEIZSÄCKER, Apostolic Age of the Christian Church, Vol. I, pp. 94–98 ; RAMSAY, St. Paul the Traveler, pp. 380–382 ; NEANDER, Planting and Training of the Christian Church, Vol. I, pp. 91–98 ; Vol. II, pp. 94–104 ; FARRAR, Life and Work of St. Paul, chs. 11 to 14 ; CONYBEARE AND HOWSON, Life and Epistles of St. Paul, ch. 3.

Sec. 11.   PETER'S TOUR OF VISITATION AMONG THE CHRISTIANS OF PALESTINE.

Acts 9 : 32–43.   About 38–39 A. D.   Circuit through Palestine.

I. Study of the Facts.

Let the following subclassification of the material in this section be verified, corrected, or improved:

Par. 1. 9 : 32–35, The Healing at Lydda and its Results.

Par. 2. 9 : 36–43, The Miracle and the Ministry in Joppa.

Prepare a brief abstract of the material contained in this section.

II. Topics for Investigation.

1. *Peter's missionary activities.*— Recall what happened in 33 A. D. which spread the Christians through Palestine, and caused the formation of many Christian communities in a large number of places. What would be the duty of the apostles, as leaders in the gospel movement, toward these unnumbered local bodies of disciples? What was done in the case of the Christian converts in the city of Samaria (*cf.* Acts 8 : 14–17)? Is it probable that similar interest was shown toward the Christians in other localities? Why should Peter in particular undertake to make a tour of visitation among these scattered groups of disciples? What could he do to help them? Were the apostles perhaps frequently away from Jerusalem on such missions (*cf.* Gal. 1 : 18, 19)? When did Peter set out upon this tour? How long a time may we suppose it to have occupied? Can we at all trace the route which he took? Where do we find him at the close of the tour? How long did he remain at Joppa (*cf.* vs. 43)? How was this journey of Peter's like, and how different from, the missionary journeys by which Paul at a later time spread the gospel through Asia and Greece?

2. *The miracles at Lydda and Joppa.*— Indicate upon the map the location of Lydda, Sharon, and Joppa. How had Christianity been introduced into these places? Note the use in vss. 13, 32, and 41 of this chapter of the term "saints" to designate the disciples; was it a common designation, and what was the significance of it? Consider Peter's miracle-working as a part of his missionary activity. Was

Æneas one of the Lydda Christians?   Was palsy a common affliction
among the Jews in the first century (*cf.* Matt. 4 : 24 ; 8 : 6 ; 9 : 2–6 ;
Acts 8 : 7)?   Compare with the healing of Æneas the somewhat similar
cure performed by Jesus (Mark 2 : 1–12).   Observe the words of Peter
in invoking the cure (vs. 34).   What was the result of the healing of
Æneas upon the people of the village?   What was the chief purpose
of the miracle?   How far from Lydda was Joppa?   What is told
about the character and life of Tabitha?   Why is the Greek meaning
of her name noted in the Acts?   When did her death take place (vs.
37)?   Why was Peter sent for—was it for the comfort and sympathy
of his presence, or with the hope that he would restore her to life?
Observe the indications of oriental funeral customs in vss. 37, 39.
Why are the "widows" particularly mentioned (vss. 39, 41)?   Why
was not Jesus' name used in raising Tabitha as in the former cure (vs.
40 ; *cf.* vs. 34)?   What was the purpose of this miracle?   What was its
effect upon the people of Joppa?   Compare with this miracle of restoration the raising of Jairus' daughter by Jesus (Mark 5 : 22, 23,
38–42).

   3. *Peter's preparation for his coming experience.*—In what ways
would this extended tour among the Palestinian Christians prepare
Peter for a larger and higher view of Christianity?   In view of Jewish
abhorrence of the tanner's trade, what does Peter's long stay with
Simon the tanner (vs. 43) indicate as to his relation to Jewish ceremonialism?   As a Galilean was he comparatively free from such scruples,
although observing the essential restrictions regarding the clean and
unclean?   Was Peter, as compared with the other apostles, the one
best fitted to comprehend and to carry forward the universal gospel as
taught by Christ and now to be retaught him by special revelation in
Joppa and special illustration in Cæsarea?

III. OBSERVATIONS AND TEACHINGS.

   1. *Organization.*—Peter made a missionary tour among the local
bodies of disciples in Palestine, for the purpose of assisting them and
directing them in their organization, internal Christian life, and evangelizing work.

   2. *Environment.*—The inhabitants of Lydda and Joppa were in
sympathy with the Christians and many converts were made by Peter's
miracles among them.

   3. *Institutions.*—Kneeling to pray seems to have been one of the
customary religious forms among the primitive Christians.

4. *Belief and teaching.*—Jesus Christ was the source of the miraculous healing, and many were led to believe in him because of it.—Peter manifested in conduct and disposition a readiness to receive the divine revelation which was about to be given him.

5. *Daily .ife.*—Miracle-working was still a part of the apostolic activity and a means of large accessions to the gospel.—The Acts narrative leaves Paul at work in Cilicia while it turns to note the preparation of Peter for his experience with Cornelius.

6. *Divine guidance.*—The gospel was greatly advanced in Lydda and Joppa by God's manifest presence among them in the healing of Æneas and the restoration of Tabitha to life.—The saintly character and useful life of Tabitha were still more impressed upon all by her living again among them.

Literature.—Upon this section see the commentaries on Acts, especially those of GLOAG, HACKETT, MEYER, and the CAMBRIDGE BIBLE. Also BIBLE DICTIONARY, articles Æneas, Dorcas, Joppa, Lydda, Peter. Only the briefest mention of these incidents is made in other books than the commentaries.

Sec. 12. PETER RETAUGHT THE FREEDOM OF CHRISTIANITY FROM JUDAISM.

Acts 10: 1–48.   About 40 A. D.   Joppa, Cæsarea.

I. STUDY OF THE FACTS.

Let the following subclassification of the material in this section be verified, corrected or improved :

Par. 1. 10 : 1–8,   The Divine Communication to Cornelius.

Par. 2. 10 : 9–16,   The Divine Communication to Peter.

Par. 3. 10 : 17–23a, Peter and the Messengers of Cornelius.

Par. 4. 10 : 23b–23, Peter's Mission to Cæsarea.

Par. 5. 10 : 34–43, Peter's Address to Cornelius and his Friends.

Par. 6. 10 : 44–48, Gentiles Received as such into Christian Fellowship.

1. Prepare a brief abstract of the material contained in this section, noting the chief facts and recounting them in your own language.

2. Write out a careful paraphrase of Peter's address (vss. 34–43), reproducing as exactly as possible the thought and the spirit of the text.

II. TOPICS FOR INVESTIGATION.

1. *Cornelius and his vision.*—Locate Cæsarea upon the map, and learn something about the city as it was at that time. Ascertain what can be known about Cornelius, as to his nationality, his official position, and the occasion of his residence in Cæsarea. Look up other New Testament references to centurions. What information is given as to his character and religious life (*cf.* vss. 2, 22)? Explain vs. 4, last clause (*cf.* vs. 31). What was his relation to the religion of the Jews? Were such as he peculiarly prepared for receiving the gospel ? Was Cornelius somewhat acquainted with the facts of Christ's life (*cf.* vss. 37, 38)? State the circumstances under which the vision was given to Cornelius. What was the substance of the vision ? What was the nature of it ? What was the purpose of it ? Why was a supernatural communication necessary in this instance ? Compare with each other the four accounts of this vision (10 : 3–6, 22, 30–33; 11: 13, 14), noting and explaining any divergences in the reports. Why does the narrator dwell at so much length, and with so much repetition, upon this incident ?

2. *The revelation to Peter.*—What were the circumstances under which Peter also received a divine communication ?   Note the oriental customs alluded to in vs. 9, last clause.   Compare the account of this in 10 : 9–16 with that given in 11 : 5–10, explaining the variations. What was the difference between a trance (vs. 10, *ekstasis*) and a vision (vs. 3, *horama*)?   Consider how this special manifestation to Peter corresponds to and complements that given Cornelius.   What was the substance of Peter's trance?   Note that it attaches to Peter's natural condition of hunger.   Why must Peter be taught this truth of the universal and spiritual nature of the gospel in this special way?   When did the meaning of the revelation become clear to him?   Before the trance, what was Peter's position regarding the clean and the unclean, and why (*cf.* Lev. 11; Deut. 14 ; Dan. 1 : 8–12)?   When did this ceremonial legislation arise among the Jews ?   What was the purpose of such distinctions and restrictions?   What had been Jesus' teaching regarding them (*cf.* Mark 7 : 1–10)?   Why was the whole system superseded by Christianity?   Compare Paul's teaching upon this matter (*cf.* Rom. 2 : 28, 29; 14 : 14).   How was it possible for the apostles, and for the most part the disciples, to fail so completely in apprehending Jesus' emphatic and clear condemnation of Jewish ceremonialism ?

3. *Peter's address to Cornelius and his friends.*— Consider the following analysis of Peter's speech : *a*) a declaration that Christianity is for all who will; *b*) an appeal for its acceptance by preaching Jesus, as to his person, his work, his death, his resurrection, and his exaltation ; *c*) a prophetical substantiation of this; *d*) an announcement of redemption and forgiveness of sins through Christ.   Should it be inferred from 10 : 44 ; 11 : 15 that Peter was interrupted in his speech by the coming of the Spirit upon them, so that he did not finish what he had intended to say?   Compare Peter's address on this occasion with those previously recorded of him (*cf.* 2 : 14–36; 3 : 12–26; 4 : 8–12; 5 : 29–32), and observe what is peculiar to this address.   Consider carefully all of Peter's statements about Jesus in his words to Cornelius. What is Peter's teaching in vss. 34, 35 concerning the relation of the devout and good Gentiles to God — that they are acceptable without becoming Christians, or that they are peculiarly ready for Christianity (*cf.* Rom. 10 : 12, 13)?   How does vs. 43 stand in doctrinal relation with vss. 34, 35 ?   Observe how Peter adapts his argument to his hearers, subordinating the argument from Jewish prophecy because those to whom he spoke were Gentiles.

4. *The Gentile Pentecost.*—Observe that Peter in 11:17 regards this impartation of the Holy Spirit to the Gentiles as parallel with that of Pentecost to the Jews (Acts 2). Compare the two events as to time, circumstances, phenomena, and importance. Why in this case did the Spirit baptism precede the water baptism? Did the latter indicate the acceptance of these Gentile converts into the Christian fellowship of the disciples, while the former indicated their acceptance by God? Why were they not baptized into the Father, Son, and Holy Ghost (vs. 48, *cf.* Matt. 28 : 19)? Previous to this Cornelius event, what was the conception of the apostles as to the salvation of the Gentiles? How was this different from Christ's conception, and why? How came it that this tremendous truth of the gospel was not developed and enforced by Christ himself, but was left for the primitive Christians to realize? Was the question of admitting Gentiles directly into Christianity without conformity to Judaism faced by Peter for the first time at Cæsarea? Why was Peter divinely chosen to decide this important matter? What light had already been thrown upon the problem by the preaching of Stephen? Explain how a step in this direction had already been taken by the apostles in their recognition of the Samaritan Christians.

III. OBSERVATIONS AND TEACHINGS.

1. *Organization.*—Up to this point all the disciples had been Jews either by birth or by adoption; now, in the case of Cornelius and his friends, Gentiles were admitted as such into Christian fellowship.

2. *Environment.*—Cornelius was one of a large class of Gentiles who, disgusted with their national pagan religions, had accepted the spiritual religion of the Jews as worthier and more satisfactory; yet he and his class were anxious for some form of religion still better, as their interest in Christianity attested.

3. *Institutions.*—The observance of the Jewish ceremonial law was a feature of the life of most of the Christians, though it may be inferred that the followers of Stephen were free from it.—The new Gentile converts were baptized in the name of Jesus Christ.

4. *Belief and teaching.*—Previous to the Cornelius event all of the apostles and the great body of disciples held that, while the gospel was also for and should be preached to the Gentiles, nevertheless they could become Christians only after they had become Jews by submitting to the rite of circumcision and conforming to Jewish customs in general.— This was not Jesus' teaching, and Stephen had attacked its externalism;

by Peter's experience with Cornelius he was led to see and acknowledge that the gospel was universal and spiritual.

5. *Daily life.*—Peter was accompanied upon this occasion by six Jewish Christians from Joppa who acted as witnesses, advisers, and assistants in this critical experience.

6. *Divine guidance.*—The Holy Spirit was imparted to the Gentile converts with much the same circumstance and impressiveness as to the Jewish converts on the day of Pentecost.—The time had come, in God's providence, for an expansion of the gospel which would embrace both Jews and Gentiles, and on an equal footing.—Peter was sinedpir to declare that Christianity was for all, independently of Judaism, and he preached Jesus in the essential aspects of his person and work.

Literature.—Upon this section see the commentaries on Acts, especially those of GLOAG, HACKETT, MEYER, and the CAMBRIDGE BIBLE. Also McGIFFERT, History of Christianity in the Apostolic Age, pp. 101-108; WEIZSÄCKER, Apostolic Age of the Christian Church, Vol. I, pp. 103, 104; NEANDER, Planting and Training of the Christian Church, Vol. I, pp. 66-76; Vol. II, pp. 81-87; FARRAR, Life and Work of St. Paul, chap. 15; CONYBEARE AND HOWSON, Life and Epistles of St. Paul, chap. 4; STIFLER, Introduction to the Book of Acts, sec. ix; BIBLE DICTIONARY, articles Cæsarea, Centurion, Cornelius, House, Peter, Unclean Meats, Vision.

Acts 11 : 1–18.   About 40 A. D.   Jerusalem.

I. Study of the Facts.

Let the following subclassification of the material in this section be verified, corrected, or improved :

Par. 1. 11: 1–3, Peter Called to Account by the Jerusalem Christians.

Par. 2. 11: 4–17, His Report and Defense of his Reception of Cornelius.

Par. 3. 11: 18,   Concurrence of Jerusalem Christians in Peter's Action.

Prepare a brief abstract of the material contained in this section.

II. Topics for Investigation.

1. *The self-justification of Peter.*—Was Peter summoned to Jerusalem to explain his action, or was his return simply awaited ? Trace upon the map the route which Peter would probably take in returning from Cæsarea to Jerusalem. In view of Peter's patient, painstaking presentation of the matter, what importance did he consider it to have ? Was his simple narration of his divinely arranged experience the best calculated to carry conviction and acceptance of the newly developed truth?' How was he supported by the six Joppa witnesses who had been at Cæsarea, and were now present at Jerusalem (vs. 12, *cf.* 10: 23)? Compare carefully the account in vss. 5–14 with the parallel account in chap. 10, explaining such variations as appear. Consider Peter's syllogistic argument in vss. 16, 17 : *a)* the disciples of Jesus were to receive the baptism of the Holy Spirit ; *b)* the Gentiles had received that baptism ; *c)* therefore the Gentiles were disciples. How does Peter regard this event as compared with the Jewish Pentecost of Acts 2 ? What was Peter's conclusion from this Cornelius experience ? How did this differ from his previous conceptions ?

2. *Concurrence of the Jerusalem Christians.*— Exactly what was the ground of the objections raised against Peter's relations to Cornelius? Explain in detail the meaning and allusions of vs. 3 (*cf.* Acts 10 : 28 ; Mark 2 : 16). Who were the persons who found fault with Peter (explain the phrase (vs. 2) "they that were of the circumcision")? What proportion of the Jerusalem Christians joined in this condemna-

tion? What previous experiences should have prepared them, and in some measure did prepare them, for this admission to Christianity of Cornelius and his friends (*cf.* chaps. 6, 7, 8, 9)? What was the effect of Peter's argument in defense of his Cæsarean action upon the Jerusalem Christians? As recognized leader in the Christian movement would his influence be very great? What then was the decision of the Jerusalem Christians regarding Peter's admission of Cornelius and his friends to full Christian fellowship? Was this decision regarded as establishing a principle and precedent, or was the Cornelius case looked upon as exceptional (compare the attitude of the Jerusalem Christians ten years later as it appears in Acts 15)?

III. Observations and Teachings.

1. *Organization.*—The Jerusalem Christians concur heartily in the reception of the Gentiles, Cornelius and his friends, into Christian fellowship.

2. *Environment.*—Does the present section contribute any information on this subject?

3. *Institutions.*—Some of the Christians were exceedingly tenacious of their Jewish notions about the ceremonially clean and unclean, while perhaps the larger portion were inclined to liberality in the matter, though quite unwilling to abandon the system.

4. *Belief and teaching.*—Peter's simple presentation of the facts, supported by the testimony of his six Jewish-Christian companions from Joppa, persuaded the Christians of Jerusalem to recognize the Gentile converts, and at least for this one instance to admit the principle that Christianity was independent of Judaism.

5. *Daily life.*—The deliberative action and wise decision in the Cornelius matter were the forerunners of the great conference at Jerusalem ten years later.

6. *Divine guidance.*—The argument from experience is the great argument for any truth; God leads men through and by means of their experiences.

Literature.—The same as that cited under the previous section, which see.

SEC. 14. FIRST MENTION OF THE GENTILE-CHRISTIAN COM-
MUNITY AT ANTIOCH (FOUNDED SOON AFTER 33 A. D.).

Acts 11: 19–30.   About 40–45 A. D.   Antioch.

I. STUDY OF THE FACTS.

Let the following subclassification of the material in this section
be verified, corrected, or improved:

Par. 1. 11: 19–21, The Beginning of the Gospel in Antioch.

Par. 2. 11: 22–26, Growth of the Church, Barnabas and Paul Leaders.

Par. 3. 11: 27–30, Antioch Christians Assist their Brethren in Judea.

Prepare a careful abstract of the facts recorded in this section.

II. TOPICS FOR INVESTIGATION.

1. *Establishment of Christianity in Antioch.*—Does vs. 19 follow in
time immediately upon the preceding section, so that the introduction
of Christianity into Antioch came in the year 40 or 41 A. D.; or, does
vs. 19 connect chronologically with Acts 8 : 1, 4, so that the gospel missionaries reached Antioch very soon after the death of Stephen, therefore in 33 or 34 A. D.? Ascertain something about the city of Antioch
at this time—its location, size, nationalities among its population,
political relations, general religious condition. Observe two classes of
gospel missionaries who reached Antioch—those who would present
the gospel only to Jews, and those of Cyprus and Cyrene who preached
to the Gentiles also. Consider carefully the variant reading in vs. 20,
"Greeks," mg. rdg. "Grecian Jews," and show from the context how
the text reading is the correct one. Why this difference of policy
between the two classes of missionaries in Antioch? Which class had
the greater success, and why? What was the importance of this step
—the giving of the gospel to the Gentiles without requiring them to
conform to Jewish rites and customs? How came these missionaries
to take it—had they teaching to that effect from Jesus and Stephen,
or had they any precedent for this action?

2. *The Antioch church and the Jerusalem church.*—How long after
the introduction of the gospel into Antioch before word reached Jerusalem that a Gentile-Christian church was growing up there?
Although the Christians of Antioch were mainly Gentiles, were there
also Jews among them (*cf.* Gal. 2 : 11–13)? Why would the Jerusalem

church be especially interested in the Antioch church? What was their purpose in sending to Antioch a delegate or representative (*cf.* Acts 8:14–17)? Why was Barnabas chosen for this mission (*cf.* Acts 4:36, 37; 9:27)? How did he find things in Antioch? Why was he so willing to recognize the legitimacy and success of the new practice of offering the gospel directly to the Gentiles, regardless of Judaism? Would the Jerusalem church as readily agree to the new movement? Why is no mention made of Barnabas' report to the Jerusalem church, and its action? Who was secured to assist in the work at Antioch? Why was he chosen? In what year was this? Where was Paul, and how engaged, at the time that he was called to work in the Antioch church? Had he had any previous relation to this church, anything to do with the founding of it? Was the Antioch church henceforth to be the center of and leader in the Gentile-Christian movement? What new name for the "disciples" grew up at Antioch? Did the name originate with the Gentiles rather than with the Jews or with the disciples themselves? Compare Acts 26:28; 1 Peter 4:16, the only other occurrences of the title "Christians" in the New Testament. Was the new name a naturally formed one (compare "Herodians" to denote the followers of Herod) for distinguishing the disciples from other religious bodies?

3. *Prophets and elders among the primitive Christians.*—Is this the first mention (vs. 27) of prophets in the Acts? When did they arise? What particular service did they render (*cf.* Acts 2:17; 13:1; 15:32; 19:6; 21:10, 11; Rom. 12:6; 1 Cor. 12:28, 29; 13:2, 8; 14:22–40)? Was prediction of future events a part of their work; if so, to what extent? Why did prophets from Jerusalem go down to Antioch in 43 or 44 A. D.? Consider Agabus' prediction of the famine (*cf.* Acts 21:10, 11); what was the purpose of the prediction? Ascertain what you can about the famine which came a little later, perhaps in 45 or 46 A. D. Was the extent of the famine correctly stated in vs. 28 ("over all the world")? What did the disciples in Antioch do for their Jerusalem brethren? How could the Antioch Christians spare the relief which they sent to Judea? How was this assistance sent? Why were Barnabas and Paul the bearers of it? To whom in Jerusalem did they deliver it? Note that we have in vs. 30 the first mention of elders among the primitive Christians. What seems from this passage to have been their function as church officers? Were they the ruling officers in each church? Had each church one only, or several? When and how did the formal office of elder in the Christian organiza-

tion arise? Was it perhaps after the dispersion of the Christians from
Jerusalem, when there grew up Christian communities in many places, and
there came the need for local governing officers? What authority had the
elders? Was there at this time any other formal office among the Christians except that of deacons (Acts 6 : 1–6) and elders? Compare the
Christian office of elder with the similar office in the Jewish synagogue.

III. OBSERVATIONS AND TEACHINGS.

1. *Organization.*—The prophets among the primitive Christians
were a class of inspired teachers of the gospel, to whom the power of
prediction was sometimes given ; they were not formal church officers.
—The formal office of elder in the organization of the Christian
churches is incidentally mentioned ; the elders were probably the ruling
officers in the local communities of Christians, presumably several to
each such community, and exercising an authority delegated by the
local body of Christians of which they were the officers.

2. *Environment.*—Hellenistic Christians, soon after the dispersion
from Jerusalem, presented the gospel to the Gentiles in Antioch independently of Judaism, and their labors won large and significant success.

3. *Institutions.*—The title of Christians was about this time given by
the Gentiles to the disciples of Christ, a simple distinguishing term
constructed after the Roman manner of forming appellations.

4. *Belief and teaching.*—It was Hellenistic Christians, probably the
followers of Stephen, who practically put into effect at Antioch the
universal idea of the gospel, which made it a religion not only for Jews
but equally for Gentiles without conformity to Judaism.

5. *Daily life.*—The Antioch disciples showed a true Christian spirit
of brotherhood in sending relief to their Jerusalem brethren who were
in distress because of the famine.

6. *Divine guidance.*—The courageous advance into the realization of
the universal gospel was inspired, guided, and richly blessed by God.—
It was only slowly, through many years, that Paul was being prepared
for and started upon his great career as the missionary of the Gentiles.

Literature.—Upon this section see the commentaries on Acts, especially those of
GLOAG, HACKETT, MEYER, and the CAMBRIDGE BIBLE. Also McGIFFERT, History
of Christianity in the Apostolic Age, pp. 108–112 ; WEIZSÄCKER, Apostolic Age of the
Christian Church, Vol. I, pp. 104–108 ; RAMSAY, St. Paul the Traveler, pp. 48–51 ;
NEANDER, Planting and Training of the Christian Church, Vol. I, pp. 99–101 ; FARRAR,
Life and Work of St. Paul, chap. 16 ; CONYBEARE AND HOWSON, Life and Epistles
of St. Paul, chap. 4 ; STIFLER, Introduction to the Book of Acts, sec. x ; BIBLE DIC-
TIONARY, articles Agabus, Antioch, Barnabas, Claudius, Cyprus, Cyrene, Elders,
Phœnicia, Prophets.

SEC. 15. PERSECUTION OF THE JERUSALEM CHRISTIANS
BY HEROD.

Acts 12:1–25.   44 A. D.   Jerusalem.

I. STUDY OF THE FACTS.

Let the following subclassification of the material in this section be
verified, corrected, or improved :

Par. 1. 12 : 1, 2,   Martyrdom of the Apostle James.
Par. 2. 12 : 3–10,   Frustrated Attempt to put Peter to Death.
Par. 3. 12 : 11–17,   Peter Withdraws for Safety from Jerusalem.
Par. 4. 12 : 18–23,   Herod's Self-Glorification and Death.
Par. 5. 12 : 24, 25, Growth of the Gospel and Return of the
                      Antioch Delegates.

Prepare a careful abstract of the facts recorded in this section.

II. TOPICS FOR INVESTIGATION.

1. *The martyr death of James the apostle.*—The deeds and death of
Herod recorded in Acts 12 took place in the year 44 A. D.; this date
is fixed by Josephus, and is perhaps the most certain date in the Acts
history. The famine mentioned in 11 : 27–30, and the consequent
visit of Barnabas and Paul, could not have come until a year or two
later, 45 or 46 A. D. Consider then that chap. 12 does not follow
chronologically upon chap. 11, and that between vss. 23 and 25 of
chap. 12 there intervenes one year or two. Which one of the Herods
is this (vs. 1) ? What was his relation to the Romans, to the Jews, and
to the Christians ? Why did he undertake this persecution of Christianity (*cf*. vs. 3)? Explain the fact that it is not now the Jewish
religious leaders, but the Jewish civil ruler, who is the persecutor.
Why did he choose James as his first victim ? Which James was this
—the apostle (Matt. 4 : 21), or the brother of Jesus (*cf*. vs. 17) ? Do
we know anything about him in the period between Jesus' ascension
and his own martyrdom ; if not, why not ? Why does the martyr
death of James receive such brief mention in Acts ? On James'
martyrdom compare Matt. 20 : 20–23. What was the effect of his
death upon the Christians ?

2. *The deliverance and withdrawal of Peter.*—Why was it at the
Passover season (vss. 3, 4) that Herod began his persecution (*cf*. vs. 11,
last clause) ? Did he intend to put Peter also to death ? State briefly

the facts of Peter's imprisonment and providential deliverance. What was the nature and the amount of the miraculous involved in this? Why has so extended an account of this event been given? Was Peter's release in answer to the prayer of his fellow-Christians (vs. 5)? What was the feeling of the primitive Christians with reference to God's care and provision for them? State briefly what Peter did after his release. Why were the disciples gathered at Mary's house? What was Peter's message to them? Why did he leave Jerusalem? Compare with this his action at an earlier time, Acts 5 : 17–23. Compare Paul's action, Acts 9 : 23–25. Whither did Peter go from the city? How long was he absent, and what was he doing during his absence?

3. *Herod's self-glorification and death.*—Ascertain the main facts as to the number, the nationality, the business, and the characteristics of the people of Tyre and Sidon. What relations did they at this time sustain to Judea? Why was Herod displeased with them? How was their country dependent upon Palestine (*cf.* 1 Kings 5 : 1–12; Ezek. 27 : 16, 17)? Had Herod shown his displeasure by restricting their commerce with his own country? What was the mission of the embassy? On what occasion did Herod publicly receive the ambassadors from Tyre and Sidon? Did he probably decide the matter in their favor, since his own subjects were pleased, and they would not like their trade relations disturbed? Compare the account of this event given by Josephus (*Jewish Antiquities*, 19, 8, 2; also 18, 6–8), which supplements Luke's account. Observe that this matter of the Phœnician embassy is introduced into the Acts narrative to show Herod's inordinate passion for display and the praise of men (*cf.* vss. 21, 22). What is known as to the previous career and the character of Herod Agrippa I? Was this act of self-glorification in keeping with them? Consider the cause and the nature of the disease with which he was smitten. How soon did his death follow? Compare Josephus' account of his death (*Jewish Antiquities*, 8, 2). Is this miserable death of Herod to be looked upon as a divine judgment against him for his vanity and cruelty? Consider the death from a similar cause of Antiochus Epiphanes (2 Macc. 9 : 9), Herod the Great (Josephus' *Jewish Antiquities*, 17, 6, 5), Philip II, of Spain, and others (see Camb. Bible, *in loc.*)

4. *Condition of Christianity in 44 A. D.*—Observe that the Book of Acts is divided into two main sections, the first section closing with chap. 12. In this portion Peter has been the chief figure, Jerusalem the center, and Palestine mainly the field of Christianity. In the sec-

ond section of Acts, from chap. 13 to the end, Paul will be the chief figure, Antioch the center, and the Gentile world the field of Christianity. After chap. 12 Peter does not again appear in the history except at the Jerusalem conference in chap. 15. It will be desirable, therefore, to note the condition of Christianity at this time. What was its territorial extent? Which were the great centers of Christian activity? Who were the prominent workers? What was the environment of the church at this time as to the Pharisees, Sadducees, common people, and civil power? How did Herod's persecution differ from former ones? What was the status of Christianity as to numbers and influence? What was the attitude and practice of the Christians at this time regarding the admission of Gentiles to Christianity?

III. OBSERVATIONS AND TEACHINGS.

1. *Organization.*—Does the present section contribute any information on this subject?

2. *Environment.*—Herod conducted this short but severe persecution of the Christians out of a desire to ingratiate himself with the Jews and with a spirit of sheer cruelty.

3. *Institutions.*—A meeting of Christians for special prayer for Peter, and presumably for themselves, was held at night for safety; such meetings afterward became common, for safety and for their special solemnity.

4. *Belief and teaching.*—The faithful, united prayer of Christ's disciples prepares the way for marked manifestations of God's presence and blessing.—Christian wisdom enjoins prudence and self-preservation except in special emergencies; the apostles repeatedly fled from danger which threatened them.

5. *Daily life.*—James the apostle seems to have been the first of the Twelve to die as a martyr.—Peter was miraculously delivered from a similar fate at the same time.

6. *Divine guidance.*—The deliverance of Peter is fully and vividly described as a testimony to God's care and provision for his children. —In spite of persecution Christianity was growing mightily in extension, influence, and numbers.

Literature.—Upon this section see the commentaries on Acts, especially those of GLOAG, HACKETT, MEYER, and the CAMBRIDGE BIBLE. Also MCGIFFERT, History of Christianity in the Apostolic Age, p. 93; NEANDER, Planting and Training of the Christian Church, Vol. I, pp. 101–105; FARRAR, Life and Work of St. Paul, chap. 17; CONYBEARE AND HOWSON, Life and Epistles of St. Paul, chap. 4; STIFLER, Introduction to the Book of Acts, sec. xi; BIBLE DICTIONARY, articles Angels, Herod, James, Mark, Prison, Sidon, Tyre.

SEC. 16. PAUL'S FIRST EVANGELIZING TOUR.

Acts 13 : 1—14 : 28.   About 46–48 A. D.   Antioch, Cyprus, Galatia

I. STUDY OF THE FACTS.

Let the following subclassification of the material in this section be verified, corrected, or improved :

Par. 1. 13 : 1–3,   Appointment of Barnabas and Saul as Missionaries.

Par. 2. 13 : 4–12,   Missionary Work in the Island of Cyprus.

Par. 3. 13 : 3,   Withdrawal of John Mark from the Company.

Par. 4. 13 : 14, 15,   Reception of Paul and Barnabas at Pisidian Antioch.

Par. 5. 13 : 16–41,   Paul's Discourse in the Synagogue.

Par. 6. 13 : 42–52,   Labors in and Expulsion from Antioch.

Par. 7. 14 : 1–7,   Work of Paul and Barnabas in Iconium.

Par. 8. 14 : 8–10,   The Healing of the Cripple at Lystra.

Par. 9. 14 : 11–18,   Paul and Barnabas taken for Pagan Gods.

Par. 10. 14 : 19–20a,   Paul Severely but not Fatally Stoned.

Par. 11. 14 : 20b–25,   Revisitation of the Churches Established on the Tour.

Par. 12. 14 : 26–28,   Return to Syrian Antioch and Report to the Church.

1. Prepare a concise abstract of the material contained in this section, noting the chief facts and recounting them in your own language.

2. Write out a careful paraphrase of Paul's discourse (13 : 16–41), reproducing as exactly as possible the thought and the spirit of the text.

II. TOPICS FOR INVESTIGATION.

1. *The Antioch church and Gentile Christianity.*—Review the history of the Antioch church as recorded in Acts 11 : 19–26. With what year does chap. 13 open? Of the five prominent Antioch Christians named in vs. 1 which are prophets and which teachers? Why does Barnabas' name stand first and Paul's last? Consider the agency of the Holy Spirit (vss. 2, 4) in this important event. Observe the fasting and prayer (vss. 2, 3) in connection with it. Had the gospel interest and work of the Antioch Christians so grown that an expan-

sive movement of this kind was the next step ?   Why were Barnabas and Paul chosen for this mission ?   Why had not the Jerusalem church already undertaken the spread of the gospel among the Gentiles ? Why was the Antioch church the source and center of Gentile-Christian missions ?   How fully was the character and the route of this missionary journey arranged beforehand by the Antioch Christians ?

2. *Incidents of the work in Cyprus.*— Locate upon the map Seleucia, Cyprus, Salamis, and Paphos.   Learn what you can about the island of Cyprus.   Why was it selected as the first district for evangelization by Barnabas and Paul (*cf.* Acts 4 : 36)?   How did they reach the people with the gospel ?   How came (John) Mark to be with them (*cf.* Acts 12 : 12, 25)?   Is it to be understood from vs. 6a that the more important towns of Cyprus were visited by the missionaries ?   Ascertain the exact nature of "sorcery" or magianism as then practiced (see especially Ramsay, *St. Paul the Traveler*, pp. 75–81).   What was the character of Elymas ?   What is known about Sergius Paulus ?   What was the relation of the magian Elymas to this Roman proconsul ? Why did Sergius Paulus wish to hear the gospel presented ?   Why did Elymas attempt to prevent this ?   Consider Paul's severe rebuke, and the divine judgment upon the magian.   Compare with this the similar incident related of Peter in Acts 8 : 9–24.

3. *The itinerary of the tour and defection of Mark.*— Who appears to have been the leader of the missionary party from Antioch to Paphos ?   Why was this ?   State the circumstances which placed Paul at the head of the company (vs. 13).   Observe (vs. 9) that up to this point in the Acts Paul has been called Saul, but from this point on, Paul.   Were both names probably his from infancy, Saul a Jewish name, Paul a Gentile name, as was customary in the case of Jews who lived in Gentile lands ?   Is the change here due to the fact that Paul now left the Jewish territory, and entered upon his great lifelong work in Gentile lands, where he was always known by his Gentile name ? Who were the members of Paul's missionary company ?   Had the route beyond Cyprus been previously determined, or did Paul now determine what it should be ?   Why did he choose southeastern Asia Minor (Galatia)?   Was it the next district to the west (toward Rome) of the territory already evangelized (*cf.* Acts 9 : 30; 11 : 25; 15 : 23, 41; Gal. 1 : 21)?   Locate Perga upon the map.   Why was not the gospel preached there at this time ?   Consider Ramsay's (*St. Paul the Traveler*, pp. 89–97) hypothesis that Paul's speedy departure from Perga was due to his having contracted malarial fever there, and must

needs go inland to the highlands for recovery (the sickness referred to in Gal. 4 : 13, 14). Why was it that at this point (John) Mark left the company and returned to Jerusalem? How did Paul feel about this withdrawal (*cf.* Acts 15 : 38)? Trace upon the map the journey of the party from Perga through Antioch, Iconium, Lystra, and Derbe, and back again to Perga, Attalia, and Syrian Antioch. Ascertain what can be known about each of these towns as to location, population, social, political, and religious characteristics (see especially Ramsay, *Church in the Roman Empire*, pp. 16–58 ; *St. Paul the Traveler*, pp. 98–151). Consider the view now adopted by many scholars that these churches established on the first tour, which lay in the Roman province of Galatia, were the churches addressed in Paul's epistle to the Galatians.

4. *Paul's discourse in Pisidian Antioch.*— What two classes of people did Paul address in the synagogue (vs. 16b; *cf.* 13 : 26; 14 : 1)? Which class would be the more susceptible to the gospel message, and why? Consider the following analysis of the discourse : vss. 17–25, review of Israelitish history ; vss. 26–29, the gospel now given to the world ; vss. 30–37, Jesus' Messiahship proved by the resurrection and by the fulfilment of prophecy ; vss. 38–41, proclamation of a practical, universal gospel. What was the main point and purpose of this discourse? What was Paul's object in reviewing the Israelitish history? Compare the facts of the Old Testament history mentioned in vss. 17–22 with the Old Testament records of them (use marginal reference Bible) and account for disagreements. Compare Paul's exposition of the Old Testament history with Stephen's (Acts 7). Compare vss. 26–39 with Peter's pentecostal address (Acts 2 : 22–36). Consider the original import, and the application made here, of the four quotations (vss. 33–35, 41) from Old Testament prophecy; also the quotation in vs. 47. Consider the practical nature and the force of Paul's presention of the gospel truth. Is this the first recorded discourse of the apostle Paul? Consider carefully the features and the teachings of this discourse which are peculiarly Pauline (see especially vs. 39).

5. *Turning from Jew to Gentile with the gospel.*— Consider six reasons why Paul, wherever he went, first preached to the Jews in the synagogues : Christ directed it (Mark 7 : 27, 28 ; Matt. 10 : 5, 6 ; John 4 : 22) ; Paul preferred it (Rom. 1 : 16 ; 9 : 1 ; 11 : 11, 1 Cor. 9 : 20) ; Paul turned instinctively to his own countrymen first ; the synagogues were the most convenient places of assemblage ; they promised the

best success; they were the best channels of communication with the Gentiles, since many devout ones attended the synagogue services. Why would the gospel missionaries obtain a hearing in the synagogues? How did Paul present the gospel to the Jews, and what was his main argument for Jesus' Messiahship? What was the cause of the hostility of the Antioch Jews (Acts 13:45) against Paul and Barnabas? How did Paul meet this? Was the right of the Jews to the gospel an exclusive or only a prior right? Had Paul any precedent for presenting the gospel directly to the Gentiles? How was it received by them? Supposing the churches of the first tour to be the churches addressed in Paul's Galatian epistle, were they composed mainly of Gentiles (*cf.* Gal. 3:29; 4:8; 5:2; 6:12)? Did this abandonment of the Jews pertain only to Antioch, so that in the other places visited by Paul he preached first to the Jews, and to the Gentiles only when rejected by the Jews? How could the Jews reject the very truth and mission to which they had been divinely appointed?

6. *Gospel ministry in Iconium, Lystra, and Derbe.*—What caused the departure of Paul and Barnabas from Pisidian Antioch, and after how long a period of work? Explain the meaning (vs. 50) of "devout women of honorable estate." Why could the chief men and women of the city be stirred into opposition against the missionaries? Why did Paul and Barnabas go from there to Iconium? Who are the "disciples" referred to in vs. 52? How did Paul begin his work in Iconium? What success did he have? In what sense were some of the Jews "disobedient" (Acts 14:2)? How long a time (vs. 3) did Paul remain in Iconium? What circumstances arose which drove him from the city? Describe the healing of the cripple at Lystra. Why was this miracle performed? Compare with it the similar miracle of Peter (Acts 3:1–10). What peculiar idea of Paul and Barnabas did the Lystrans get? Why was this? What tradition existed in Lystra as to a previous visit to their city of its tutelar deities, Jupiter and Mercury? How were they about to do homage to Paul and Barnabas as gods? Why did the gospel missionaries refuse this? How did they present the true view of the matter to the people? Consider carefully Paul's words to the Lystrans on this occasion (Acts 14:15–17). What is the meaning of the saying (vs. 15) "We also are men of like passions with you"? With vs. 16 compare Rom. 1:18–25; 3:25, and explain meaning. Compare with this Lystran address the apostle's address to the Athenians (Acts 17:22–31). Who stirred up opposition

against the missionaries, and why? Why did they stone Paul? Who were the "disciples" who stood about Paul after the stoning? Are we to understand that Paul's recovery (vs. 20) was a miracle? What was the success of the work in Derbe?

7. *Revisitation and organization of the new Christians.*— Consider the wisdom and self-sacrifice of Paul in revisiting the towns of this tour instead of going directly east from Derbe through Tarsus, his home, to Antioch of Syria. What was the purpose of this revisitation? How could he return and work in those places from which he had been so recently expelled? Observe that the gospel was now preached in Perga. How much time was occupied in this revisitation? Observe in vs. 23 the second mention in Acts of "elders." What is the meaning of the Greek word *cheirotoneo* here translated "appointed"? Were these "elders" appointed in these churches by the apostles alone, or by the apostles with the approval of the church concerned, or by the church concerned with the approval of the apostles? Was there one, or more than one, elder to each church? Is it to be supposed that other officers, *e. g.*, deacons, were appointed in these churches at this time of their organization, although no mention is here made of the fact?

8. *Results of the first evangelizing tour.*—What was the relation of Paul and Barnabas to the Antioch church (*cf.* Acts 13 : 1–3)? What interest therefore would that church take in hearing an account of their missionary journey? How long a time had it been since the party set out for this work? Consider the then prevailing customs and facilities of communication between different distant districts, as to whether it is likely that any news from Paul's company had reached Antioch previous to his return. What districts had been evangelized? How many churches had been established? How many converts to Christianity had been won? Was the main outcome of the journey, however, the establishment of the principle that the gospel was for the Gentiles upon the basis of faith, without reference to Judaism? Explain the meaning of the phrase (Acts 14 : 27) "opened a door of faith unto the Gentiles" (*cf.* Acts 13 : 38, 39; 14 : 15). Discuss the turning from Jew to Gentile with the gospel, as was repeatedly found necessary on this journey. Recall the previous occasions when others had been divinely led to this same course of giving the gospel to Gentiles as well as Jews ; Peter at Cæsarea (Acts 10), and the early Christian missionaries at Antioch (Acts 11 : 19–21). Consider the relation of these experiences, leadings, and practical necessities to the conference at Jerusalem soon

to be held (Acts 15) to determine finally the relation of the Gentile to the gospel and to Judaism.

III. OBSERVATIONS AND TEACHINGS.

1. *Organization.*—The teachers in the primitive churches were a class of Christians, subordinate to apostles and prophets, who devoted themselves to giving instruction in the history and teaching of Christianity.—Paul, faithful to his mission, revisited the Asian communities where he had preached on his tour, for the purpose of confirming and organizing the new Christians into local bodies or churches.—Elders (one or more) were appointed over each church, either by the apostles or by the church with the approval of Paul and Barnabas.

2. *Environment.*—The itinerary of the missionary journey was probably not fully marked out at the start; Cyprus was naturally the first place to visit, and subsequently Paul chose southeastern Asia Minor as the district next westward to be evangelized.—The Jews, at first interested in Paul and the gospel, soon came to hate and persecute the missionaries because of their Messianic and Gentile teaching.—At Iconium, Lystra, and Derbe Paul and Barnabas worked long and successfully, as there probably were few Jews in these towns.

3. *Institutions.*—The ceremony of fasting, so common in the Old Testament history, was practiced to some extent in the primitive churches, but without the direction or the sufficient example of Christ.

4. *Belief and teaching.*—The address of Paul at Pisidian Antioch is of great interest because of its being his first recorded sermon, although he had been preaching the gospel for twelve years more or less.—The discourse has definite Pauline peculiarities, and yet his line of argument, presentation of the facts, and conception of the gospel truth, are in entire accord with, and similar to, the preaching of Peter. —At Lystra Paul and Barnabas came into contact with a quaint relic of the old paganism, in answering which Paul introduced his conception of natural religion and the philosophy of history afterwards developed more fully in Acts 17 and Rom. 1.—The great doctrinal result of the tour was the working out in practical experience of the principle that the gospel was for Gentiles as well as for Jews, upon the basis of faith, and that the Gentiles need not conform to Judaism.

5. *Daily life.*—Paul, by providential circumstance and personal qualification, became the leader of the missionary party at Paphos, as

they were about to leave Cyprus.—As from this time on he is to be the chief figure in the history, for he now enters upon his great Gentile work, Luke uses his Gentile name Paul, by which he was known among the churches and in subsequent history.—Mark withdrew from the missionary party when the inland trip from Perga was decided upon, perhaps from lack of courage to face the hardships and perils which that journey involved.—At the close of the tour a full report was made to the Antioch church which sent them out.—Paul and Barnabas probably resumed their Christian work at Antioch until they appear again a few years later at the Jerusalem conference in 50 A. D. as delegates from the Antioch church.

6. *Divine guidance.*—The Antioch church became the mother church of Gentile Christianity by reason of its systematic missionary work for extending the gospel in Gentile lands.—Barnabas and Paul, prominent workers in the Antioch church, were appointed, under the guidance of the Holy Spirit, to begin extended evangelization.—The gospel is substantially the same, whoever presents it, or wherever it is presented.

Literature.— Upon this section see the commentaries on Acts, especially those of GLOAG, HACKETT, MEYER, and the CAMBRIDGE BIBLE. Also McGIFFERT, History of Christianity in the Apostolic Age, pp. 151–160, 172–192; WEIZSÄCKER, Apostolic Age of the Christian Church, Vol. I, p. 109; RAMSAY, St. Paul the Traveler, pp. 64–151; Church in the Roman Empire, pp. 8–73; NEANDER, Planting and Training of the Christian Church, Vol. I, pp. 105–114; FARRAR, Life and Work of St. Paul, chaps. 18–21; CONYBEARE AND HOWSON, Life and Epistles of St. Paul, chaps. 5 and 6; STIFLER, Introduction to the Book of Acts, sec. xii; BIBLE DICTIONARY, articles Antioch (in Syria), Antioch (Pisidian), Attalia, Barnabas, Cyprus, Derbe, Elders, Elymas, Iconium, Jupiter, Lucius, Lycaonia, Lystra, Manaen, Mark, Mercury, Niger, Pamphylia, Paphos, Paul, Perga, Pisidia, Proconsul, Prophets, Salamis, Seleucia, Sergius Paulus.

Sec. 17. JOINT CONFERENCE AT JERUSALEM CONCERNING THE RELATION OF CHRISTIANITY TO JUDAISM.

Acts 15 : 1–35.   50 A. D.   Jerusalem.

I. Study of the Facts.

Let the following subclassification of the material in this section, with verse synopses, be verified, corrected, or improved :

Par. 1. vs. 1a, Judeans come to Antioch; vs. 1b, teaching circumcision to be essential to salvation; vs. 2a, Paul and Barnabas deny the false doctrine. Vss. 1, 2a, THE QUESTION PRESSING FOR DECISION.

Par. 2. vs. 2b, Delegates appointed to confer with the Jerusalem authorities on the matter; vs. 3, they go, preaching a universal gospel by the way; vs. 4a, they are received by the church; vs. 4b, which listens to their presentation of the case ; vs. 5, certain Pharisaic Christians again affirm the necessity of circumcision for all Christians. Vss. 2b–5, CONFERENCE OF ANTIOCH DELEGATES WITH THE JERUSALEM CHURCH.

Par. 3. vs. 6, Jerusalem authorities consider the matter; vs. 7a, much discussion results; vs. 7b, at its close Peter speaks; vs. 7c, calling to their minds the former divine revelation on this subject through his admission of Cornelius to Christianity; vs. 8, which case showed that God received Gentiles as such; vs. 9, making no distinction in favor of the Jews; vs. 10a, so why afflict the Gentiles with the burden of the ceremonial law ; vs. 10b, which was grievous even to the Jews; vs. 11, both Jew and Gentile are saved through grace. Vss. 6–11, PETER'S ADDRESS IN THE CONFERENCE.

Par. 4. vs. 12, Paul and Barnabas recount their missionary experiences with reference to the Gentiles ; vs. 13, then James, the Lord's brother, speaks; vs. 14, he refers to the choice of Israel as an intended ultimate blessing to the Gentiles; vss. 15–18, citing Old Testament prophecy to this effect; vs. 19, he commends freedom from the law, for Gentiles ; vs. 20, asking only that for expediency's sake they observe a few unessential customs; vs. 21, so that they might live harmoniously with the strict Jewish Christians. Vss. 12–21, JAMES' ADDRESS IN THE CONFERENCE.

Par. 5. vs. 22, Jerusalem Christians appoint delegates to the Antioch church; vs. 23, who should carry thither the written decree of the conference; vs. 24, in this document they repudiate responsibility for the Judean trouble makers; vss. 25, 26, commend Paul and Barnabas; vs. 27, attest their friendliness by the delegates sent; vs. 28, pronounce the law unnecessary for Gentiles; vs. 29, and enjoin a few expedient restrictions only. Vss. 22–29, DECISION AND LETTER OF THE JERUSALEM CONFERENCE.

Par. 6. vs. 30, The letter delivered to the Antioch church; vs. 31, where it causes rejoicing; vs. 32, the Jerusalem delegates affiliate cordially with the Antioch Christians; vs. 33, and then return home; vs. 35, Paul and Barnabas tarry in Antioch. Vss. 30–35, THE ANTIOCH CHURCH REJOICES AT THE SETTLEMENT OF THE GREAT QUESTION.

1. Prepare an abstract, in your own language, of the facts recorded in this section.

2. Gal. 2 : 1–10 contains another account (as most scholars think) of this same conference, an account written by Paul himself. It reveals more clearly than the Acts' narrative, because it is a first-hand report by one of the chief actors in the event, the nature of the contention and the attitude of the three parties involved. The Galatian account should therefore be carefully studied in connection with the fifteenth chapter of Acts.

II. TOPICS FOR INVESTIGATION.

1. *The occasion and problem of this conference.*—Whence came certain men (vs. 1) to Antioch? Were they members of the Jerusalem church? Did they come as representatives of that body, or as self-appointed teachers (vs. 24)? Exactly what was their teaching (vs. 1)? What proportion of the Jerusalem Christians shared their belief? Why did they come to Antioch to preach this doctrine? Were they the same persons, or at least of the same class, as those referred to by Paul in Gal. 2 : 4? Recall the facts about the origin and the composition of the Antioch church. Why would the teaching of these Judaistic Christians make trouble in the Antioch church? Who led in the opposition to this teaching (vs. 2)? What course of action was finally decided upon with regard to it? Consider that the question was

whether Gentiles had to conform to Judaism in order to become Christians. How had this question been raised and answered in Peter's
experience with Cornelius in Cæsarea (Acts 10)? How had it been
raised and answered in the establishment of the church in Antioch
(Acts 11:19–24)? How had it been raised and answered on Paul's
first missionary journey (Acts 13:44–49)? How did these preliminary experiences and decisions foreshadow and influence this final
decision of the question by the Jerusalem conference?

2. *The constitution and authority of the conference.*— Why did the
Antioch church show such deference to the Jerusalem church in this
matter? Besides these two churches, were there any others represented
in this conference? If not, why not? Considering the composition
of the body, ought it to be called a "council"? Contrast this meeting
with later "councils" of the Christian church. What authority had
this company—the Jerusalem Christians and some delegates from
Antioch—to decide this question? Were the leaders of the Christian
movement all present on this occasion? What weight would the decision have with all the churches?

3. *The proceedings of the conference.*—From a careful examination
of Acts 15:4–6 determine whether more than one meeting is referred
to. If two meetings are mentioned, were both full public meetings?
Observe that Gal. 2:2 speaks only of a private conference of Paul and
the other delegates with the leading Jerusalem apostles. Was this a
third meeting, not mentioned in the Acts; or are the two accounts of
the conference in some disagreement? In the latter case is Paul's
account to be followed, as being a first-hand report of the proceedings? In the former case were there three meetings: (*a*) a general
reception by the whole church, with reports by Paul and Barnabas of
their Gentile work, and objection made by the Pharisaic Christians
(Acts 15:4); (*b*) a private conference to arrange matters between the
leaders (Gal. 2:2): (*c*) a second full, public meeting for final discussion and decision (Acts 15:6)? Observe the order of procedure
in the final meeting: much debate, Peter's address, reports by Paul
and Barnabas, James' address, the decision, the written decree, the
appointment of delegates to. Antioch. What relation did James sustain to this conference? How did the conference arrive at and
formulate its decision?

4. *The three parties in the conference* —Consider that there were three
parties in the conference, representing different views which must be

adjusted to one another; the Pharisaic Christians, the Gentile Christians, and the Jewish Christians. What was the opinion of the Pharisaic Christians (*cf.* Acts 15 : 5)—that no Gentile should be admitted to
Christianity except throught the gateway of Judaism? What was the
opinion of the Gentile Christians (*cf.* Gal. 2 : 1–10)—that they should
be entirely exempt from the Jewish law? What was the opinion of
the Jewish Christians (*cf.* Acts 15 : 10, 11, 19)—that though they would
have preferred to see all Christians conform to Judaism, yet it was evident from previous experience that this could not be demanded, and
so freedom from Judaism was conceded the Gentile Christians, while it
remained obligatory upon the Jewish Christians? Do we know the
names of any of the Pharisaic Christian leaders? Who were the Gentile Christian leaders? Who were the Jewish Christian leaders? Why
was it impossible for the Pharisaic Christian opinion to prevail? What
were the reasons which led the Jewish Christians to concede to the
Gentile Christians immunity from Judaism? Study carefully the
account in Gal. 2 : 1–10 as to the relation of Paul to Peter, James,
and John in this conference. What right had Paul to claim equal
authority with them? Did they concede all that Paul asked for at this
time? What distribution of the missionary field was made? Were
the Pharisaic Christians persuaded to acquiesce, or were they simply
suppressed?

5. *The addresses of Peter and James.*—Consider Peter's address as
the closing of the general discussion of the matter. To what important historical event did he direct their attention (*cf.* Acts 10 and 11)?
Why had not the influence of this event had a greater effect upon the
Jerusalem Christians? Could Peter do otherwise than stand firmly
upon this former experience? What did he affirm to be the one only
condition of salvation? In view of this, what did he recommend?
Consider James' address as the final speech of the conference. Did
any peculiar authority attach to James' judgment on the question?
Explain the Old Testament passage cited, as to its original use
and its application here. What opinion did James express as to
how the problem should be settled? State and explain the restrictions which James attached to the liberty which he conceded (vss.
20, 21).

6. *The decision and letter of the conference.*—Was James' opinion
made the decision of the conference? State then what the decision
was. Why has Paul made no mention, in Gal. 2 or elsewhere, of the
restrictions which were laid upon the Gentiles? Give reasons for

believing that vss. 23–29 contain the exact decree as sent out by the Jerusalem conference. How was this letter carried to and received by the Antioch Christians? Consider that the Jerusalem agreement, while releasing the Gentile Christians from Judaism, took it for granted that the Jewish Christians would continue in their Judaism. Would it be possible for Jewish and Gentile Christians to live in true Christian brotherhood with the barrier of the Jewish law between them? Would this difficulty assert itself in almost every church? Can the Jerusalem decision then be regarded as completely solving the problem? Study carefully Gal. 2 : 11–21, which records the conflict upon this point which was not decided. Was it necessary that Paul should attempt to remove this great obstruction to the gospel by getting Peter and the Jewish Christians to give up Judaism themselves also? Did he succeed in this attempt? Why has the Book of Acts practically nothing more to say about the Jerusalem Christians and the original apostles?

III. Observations and Teachings.

1. *Organization.*—No advance in the matter of church organization seems to be indicated in Acts 15 and Gal. 2. The Jerusalem church has a certain precedence due to its history, but has no more formal authority than the Antioch church, and neither of them has any formal authority over the other churches.—The elders are the only officers mentioned besides the apostles, who are the informal but acknowledged leaders of the Christian movement.

2. *Environment.*—Does the present section contribute any information on this subject?

3. *Institutions.*—The conference was a wise means for deciding a question which had for some time been prominent and vital; it was not formally official, nor was it formally representative, yet it was practically both, since all the leaders of Christianity took part in the proceedings, and agreed to abide by the decision.

4. *Belief and teaching.*—It was now conclusively established that the Gentiles should not be required to conform to Jewish rites and ceremonies, a principle which had already become practically recognized and acted upon by Peter, Paul, and others.—It remained, however, that the Jewish Christians were to continue in their Judaism.

5. *Daily life.*—What information does the present section contribute on this subject?

6. *Divine guidance.*—The problem which this conference solved was of vital importance, and a wrong decision would have divided the

primitive Christians into two strong, hostile camps.—God's providence led those in authority to a right and harmonious solution of the problem.

Literature.— Upon this section see the commentaries on Acts, especially those of GLOAG, HACKETT, MEYER, and the CAMBRIDGE BIBLE. Also McGIFFERT, History of Christianity in the Apostolic Age, pp. 192–234 ; WEIZSÄCKER, Apostolic Age of the Christian Church, Vol. I, pp. 175–216; RAMSAY, St. Paul the Traveler, pp. 152–177; SCHAFF, History of the Christian Church, Vol. I, pp. 334–360; NEANDER, Planting and Training of the Christian Church, Vol. I, pp. 109–114; Vol. II, pp. 114–128; FARRAR, Life and Work of St. Paul, chaps. 22 and 23; CONYBEARE AND HOWSON, Life and Epistles of St. Paul, chap. 7; STIFLER, Introduction to the Book of Acts, sec. xiii; BIBLE DICTIONARY, articles Barnabas, Blood, Cilicia, Circumcision, Idol, James, John, Judas (Barsabbas), Law of Moses, Peter, Silas, Syria, Synagogue, Titus.

THIRD DIVISION.

PERIOD OF GENTILE CHRISTIANITY.

Text: Acts 15: 36—28: 31.   Time: Thirteen years, 51–63 A. D.   Localities: Asia Minor, Greece, Palestine, Italy.   Leader: Paul.

The principle which had been worked out between 34 and 50 A. D. and formally recognized by the Jerusalem conference at the close of that period, that Gentile Christians were not to be required to conform to Jewish rites and customs, was firmly established during the next thirteen years, 51–63 A. D. This was the special work of the apostle Paul. The Jewish Christians in Jewish localities continued to combine Jewish rites and customs with their Christianity. In Gentile districts the Jewish Christians were in the main disposed to continue their Judaism, but as a result of Paul's strenuous and constant efforts the ceremonial barriers between Jews and Gentiles were to a large extent broken down. The gospel became established as a universal and spiritual religion, independent of Jewish rites and customs, for the reason that the greatest number of Christians were in this period Gentiles, and the most influential churches were those founded by Paul. Gentile Christianity thus prevailed over Jewish Christianity, both in numbers and in influence. It was historically true that the gospel was taken from the Jews and given to the Gentiles, although there was a host of Jewish Christians. They would have weighed the gospel down with ceremonies and limitations inconsistent with its essential liberty and breadth, so that in God's providence the gospel was put into other hands for preservation. It is the record of this great transfer and development, the narrative and the interest concerned with Gentile Christianity, which is given by the last half of the Book of Acts, and in the Pauline epistles. This third period witnesses the second and third evangelizing tours of Paul, in which his great work as an apostle of the Gentiles was principally done; then his long imprisonment in Cæsarea and Rome, with his two years' ministry in chains at the capital of the empire. The period closes with the Book of Acts, at the end of the first Roman imprisonment in 63 A. D.

SEC. 18.   PAUL'S SECOND EVANGELIZING TOUR.

Acts 15: 36—18: 22,   51-54 A. D.   Asia Minor, Greece, Antioch.

I.   STUDY OF THE FACTS.

Let the following subclassification of the material in this section be verified, corrected, or improved:

Par. 1. 15: 36–40,   Preparation for the Second Evangelizing Tour.
Par. 2. 15:41—16:5, Revisitation of Churches formerly Established.
Par. 3. 16: 6–10,   Paul Divinely Directed to Work in Macedonia.
Par. 4. 16 : 11–40,   Incidents of Paul's Labors in Philippi.

    (1) vss. 11–15, the conversion of Lydia.
    (2) vss. 16–18, the healing of the deranged girl.
    (3) vss. 19–24, Paul and Silas scourged and imprisoned.
    (4) vss. 25–34, the providential deliverance and the jailer's con-
                version.
    (5) vss. 35–40, release and departure of Paul and Silas from
                Philippi.

Par. 5. 17 : 1–9,   Work and Persecution in Thessalonica.
Par. 6. 17 : 10–15,   Brief but Successful Ministry in Berœa.
Par. 7. 17 : 16–34,   Paul's Experience in Athens.

    (1) vss. 16–22a, the religious condition of the city.
    (2) vss. 22b–31, Paul's address to the Athenians.
    (3) vss. 32–34, the small success of his efforts.

Par. 8. 18 : 1–17,   Eighteen Months of Fruitful Ministry in Corinth.

    (1) vss. 1–4,   Paul works at his trade and teaches.
    (2) vss. 5–11,   his rejection by the Jews of the city.
    (3) vss. 12–17, the arraignment of Paul before Gallio.   .

Par. 9. 18 : 18–22,   The Return to Antioch from Corinth, by Way
                of Miletus and Jerusalem.

   1. Prepare a concise abstract of the material contained in this section, noting the chief facts and recounting them in your own language.

   2. Write out a careful paraphrase of Paul's address at Athens (17 : 22–31), reproducing as exactly as possible the thought and spirit of the text.

   3. Observe the itinerary of the second evangelizing tour, and the

kind of work done: (1) Revisitation in Syria, Cilicia, and Galatia (the territory of the first tour), occupying about nine months. (2) New work in Macedonia, at Philippi, Thessalonica, and Berœa, occupying about nine months, and in Achaia, at Athens and Corinth, occupying eighteen months. (3) Return from Corinth to Antioch of Syria by way of Cenchreæ, Ephesus, Cæsarea, and Jerusalem. (4) Two epistles still extant were written on this journey, First and Second Thessalonians, a few months apart in 53 A. D., from Corinth.

II. TOPICS FOR INVESTIGATION.

1. *Paul's purpose and fellow-workers of the second tour.*— How long was it after the first tour, and how long after the Jerusalem conference, that the second tour was begun? From whom came the proposal of the first tour (*cf.* Acts 13 : 1–3), and of the second? What was Paul's idea and purpose for this tour (*cf.* Acts 15 : 36)? Did the plan and extent of the tour change after its beginning, so as to include not only revisitation, but also new work in Greece? What had he to deliver to certain churches, and which ones (*cf.* Acts 15 : 23, 41; 16 : 4)? Who constituted the party for the first tour (*cf.* Acts 13 : 2–5)? Who for the second (*cf.* Acts 15 : 36–40)? Why did not Barnabas accompany Paul on this journey? Why did Paul decline to have Mark accompany them, and was he right in so doing? Is it probable that the contention over Mark was rather superficial, while the real disagreement between Paul and Barnabas was of a fundamental doctrinal character, as indicated in Gal. 2 : 11–14? Why did Barnabas and Mark go to Cyprus for evangelizing work, and what is known of their subsequent history? Who was Silas (*cf.* Acts 15 : 22, 32, 40), and why did Paul choose him as a companion for the journey? What other fellow-workers were added to Paul's company subsequently (*cf.* Acts 16 : 1–3, Timothy; 16 : 11, Luke)?

2. *The itinerary and time of the tour.*— Indicate upon the map the territory which Paul purposed at the outset to revisit (*cf.* Acts 15 : 36, Galatia, the district of the first tour; Acts 15 : 41, Syria and Cilicia). Who had established the churches in Syria and Cilicia? Were the "decrees" (Acts 16 : 4; *cf.* 15 : 23–29) delivered to the Galatian as well as to the Syrian and Cilician churches (consider that Paul makes no mention of this in the Galatian epistle, and that Acts 16 : 4 may belong after 15 : 41)? How much time was occupied with this revisitation? How long a period was given to new work in Greece? Indicate upon the map the Greek cities in which Paul preached the gospel on

this tour.   Describe the districts of Macedonia and Achaia as to geog-
raphy, chief cities, number and classes of population, and religion.   Draw
an outline map of the territory covered by this tour, and trace upon it
Paul's journey from Antioch of Syria to Corinth.   Trace also the return
journey of Paul from Corinth by water to Ephesus and Cæsarea, and
then by land to Jerusalem and Antioch.   In what year was the return
made ?   Why is the Acts record of this second evangelizing tour so
meager as to the first part of the journey ?   Of what portions of the
tour is the account fullest, and why ?   Consider the indefiniteness of
the running notes of time, as in 15 : 41 ; 16 : 1, 4, 6; 17 : 1, 2, 10, 13,
14; 18 : 1, 11, 18, 20.

3. *Providential checks and pointings in Paul's course.*—What district
is referred to in Acts 16 : 6 as "the region of Phrygia and Galatia" (see
Ramsay's extended discussion, *Church in the Roman Empire*, pp.
74–82) on the North-Galatian hypothesis and on the South-Galatian
hypothesis ?   Why had Paul wished to work in Asia (indicate this district upon the map)?   Explain the meaning of the statement that he
was "forbidden of the Holy Ghost."   Why did Paul then turn to
Bithynia (indicate this district, and also Mysia, upon the map)?   Why
was his plan again interrupted ?   Explain the meaning of the statement that "the Spirit of Jesus suffered them not."   What was the reason for the call to Macedonia at this particular time ?   Are we to
understand that these providential checks and pointings were of the
nature of external directions or internal promptings?   Consider the'
divine assurance given Paul at Corinth (*cf.* Acts 18 : 9–11).   What other
instances were there in Paul's career of similar providential guidance ?
What is thus indicated as to God's care over the establishment of his
kingdom on earth ?

4. *The finding of Timothy and Luke.*—Was Timothy probably one
of Paul's converts on the first tour (*cf.* 1 Tim. 1 : 2)?   State the facts as
to his parentage, and his consequent relation to Juadaism.   How had
he been brought up religiously (*cf.* 2 Tim.1 : 5 ; 3: 15) ?   How old was
he when he now joined Paul's missionary company ?   Why was he
chosen by Paul for a fellow-worker (*cf.* Acts 16 : 2 ; 1 Tim. 1 : 18 ; 4 : 14;
2 Tim. 1 : 6)?   Why had not Timothy been circumcised in infancy ?
What were Paul's reasons for having him now submit to the rite (*cf.* 1
Cor. 10 : 32)?   Compare Paul's action here with his refusal to circum-
cise Titus, as recorded in Gal. 2 : 1–5.   Observe Timothy's subsequent
relation to Paul and his work (*cf.* Acts 20 : 4 ; Rom. 16 : 21 ; 1 Cor.
4 : 17 ; 2 Cor. 1 : 1 ; 1 Thess. 3 : 2, 6 ; Col. 1 : 1 ; Phile. 1 ; Phil. 1 : 1:

2 : 19; Heb. 13 : 23). Consider the significance of the pronoun "we" in Acts 16 : 10–17 (*cf.* also 20 : 5—21 : 18; 27 : 1—28 : 16). Does this indicate the accession to the missionary party of Luke, the author of the Acts? Ascertain what can be known concerning the country, nationality, age, profession, personal characteristics, and relation to Christianity of Luke. Where and how did he meet with Paul? Why did Luke join him in his work? Why is his entrance into the history given such slight notice?

5. *The results of Paul's labor in Philippi.*—Locate Philippi upon the map, and ascertain the important facts about the city as it then was —its size, inhabitants, political status, religious condition. Why did Paul begin his work in Europe here? Since there was no synagogue in Philippi, is it probable that there were but few Jews there? What was the "place of prayer" by the riverside (Acts 16 : 13)? Note and explain the fact that women are so prominently mentioned in the work at Philippi. Were the women of verse 13 Jews and Jewish proselytes? What was Lydia's religious attitude previous to her acceptance of Christianity? Why is her conversion particularly spoken of? What are we to understand was the malady of the girl who had "a spirit of divination"? Was it mental derangement or literal demoniacal possession? Explain the "soothsaying" which she was supposed to perform. How came she to give repeated testimony to the divine mission of Paul and his fellow-workers? Why was this an annoyance to Paul? Why did he not heal her at once, and why did he finally do so? How was her "soothsaying" a source of gain to her masters? What revenge did they take upon Paul and Silas for releasing the girl from her unfortunate condition? Consider the circumstances of the jailer's conversion. What was his religious condition previous to his relations with Paul and Silas? Explain the directions given him (16 : 31) as to how he might be saved. Consider these Philippian Christians as types of what the gospel was to do for pagan peoples. As to the success of Paul's work in this city compare the epistle to the Philippians, which indicates that the church he now founded here was one of the most faithful and best of all which he established.

6. *Roman persecution of the Christian missionaries.*—Was this Roman persecution of the gospel missionaries at Philippi the first (recorded) instance in which the Romans actually opposed Christianity? Who had been up to this time the instigators of, and for the most part the actors in, the uprisings against Paul and his work (*cf.* Acts 13 : 50; 14 : 2, and elsewhere)? Was this Roman hostility at Philippi directed

against the Christians as distinguished from Jews, or against Paul and
Silas as trouble-making Jews without reference to their Christianity
(*cf.* Acts 16 : 20)?   It was not then an intentional persecution of Christianity as such?   What precedent for the persecution of the Jews by
the Romans had been lately set at Rome (*cf.* Acts 18 : 2)?   Explain
the immediate occasion of the Philippian persecution.   What were
the customs set forth by Paul which it was not lawful for the
Philippians to receive or to observe (vs. 21)?   What was done with
Paul and Silas?   Why was their dismissal ordered the next morning?
Why did Paul insist (vss. 36, 37) on a formal release?   Had not
Paul made known to the authorities the day before that he and Silas
were Roman citizens?   How had Paul obtained Roman citizenship
(*cf.* Acts 22 : 25–28)?   What did such citizenship secure to a person
in Paul's position?   Why did Paul and Silas leave the city after their
release?

7. *Gospel work in Thessalonica and Berœa.*—Ascertain all that can
be known about Thessalonica and Berœa as they then were.   Why did
Paul choose to preach the gospel there?   Were there more Jews in
these two cities than there were in Philippi?   What were the three
points of Paul's teaching to the Thessalonian Jews?   How was this
teaching received by them?   Were his main converts, however, from
among the devout Gentiles?   Was the church founded here mainly
Jewish or Gentile (*cf.* 1 Thess. 1: 8–10)?   How long did Paul work in
Thessalonica?   Study the Thessalonian epistles as fully as time permits to learn of the character and success of Paul's work in Thessalonica.   Consider that he largely supported himself by manual
labor during this ministry (*cf.* 1 Thess. 2 : 9; 4 : 11; 2 Thess. 3 : 6–15).
Did he also receive money from friends (*cf.* Phil. 4 : 16)?   Recount
the circumstances under which Paul and Silas left Thessalonica.   What
was the charge made against them (Acts 17 : 6, 7; *cf.* Luke 23 : 1, 2)?
How much truth was there in it?   How different was the treatment
which Paul and Silas received at Berœa?   Why were the Jews here so
tolerant and docile?   Were there many Gentile converts also?   Is it
to be understood that a church was established at Berœa, as there had
been at Philippi and Thessalonica; if so, why is no mention made of
the fact anywhere?

8. *Paul's experience at Athens.*—Observe (Acts 17 : 16) that Paul
was only passing through Athens, it not being his intention to attempt
the establishment of the gospel here at this time; why not?   Ascertain
something about Athens as it then was, politically, socially, religiously.

Secure if possible a map of the city, and locate upon it the market place (vs. 17) and the Areopagus (vss. 19, 22). How was Paul impressed with Athens? How did he undertake to reach the citizens with the gospel while he was among them? What did they understand was the substance of his message (vs. 18)? Was Paul given a fair hearing; if so, why? What was the Areopagus, and why was Paul taken hither to give his formal presentation of Christianity to the Athenians? Consider the audience whom he addressed, as to their intellectual and religious views, their mental habit, and their capacity for taking hold of new truth. What was the purpose of Paul in his address? Make out an analysis of the thought: (1) introduction, vss. 22, 23; (2) God's relation to the material universe, vs. 24; (3) God's relation to men, vss. 25–28; (4) the nature of God, vs. 29; (5) his moral government of men, vss. 30, 31. Did Paul thus preach the unity and majesty of God, and the dependence and brotherhood of man? Observe the skill with which Paul attached his teaching to the strange altar in Athens. Consider carefully the exact meaning of "somewhat superstitious" (vs. 22, in Greek *deisidaimonesterous*, which is not well translated in the Revised Version, for the term was used by Paul in a good sense, not with reproach). What are the chief characteristics of the address? How far did the Athenians accept Paul's presentation of religious truth? To what points did they object, and why? Was it in any degree due to the manner or substance of Paul's teaching on this occasion that the gospel found no greater favor in Athens at this time? Was there a Christian church at Athens in the apostolic period?

9. *The establishment of the Corinthian church.*—Locate upon the map the city of Corinth, and ascertain something of its history previous to the Roman restoration in 46 B. C. What was the political and commercial importance of Corinth in Paul's time? What was the moral and religious condition of the city? Why did Paul select it as a field for work? State what is told about Aquila and Priscilla. Were they already Christians when Paul found them in Corinth? If so, where had they come into contact with Christianity? When and why did the Roman Emperor Claudius order the Jews to leave Rome? How long was the edict in effect? Describe Paul's trade of tent-making. Why did he work at it here in Corinth? How did Paul begin his gospel ministry in Corinth (Acts 18 : 4; *cf.* 13 : 43; 14 : 1; 17 : 1–4, 12; 18 : 19)? Explain the phrase (18 : 5) "constrained by the word." How did the Jews receive his teaching? Why were they not able to drive him out of the city, as at Thessalonica and other places? What course

did Paul pursue when rejected by the Jews ?   With Acts 18 : 6 compare 13 : 45, 46, 51.   What success had Paul among the Gentiles of
Corinth ?   What was the nature of the vision given Paul at this time
(18 : 9, 10)?   What was the purpose of the vision?   Ascertain what is
known about Gallio and his office here mentioned.   By whom, when,
and why was Paul brought before him ?   Compare Acts 16 : 19-24.
Why did Gallio refuse to hear the case ?   Was this a proper ruling,
from the point of view of Gallio's judicial office ?   Why was Sosthenes
beaten by the court officers ?   Explain the words (18 : 17) "Gallio cared
for none of these things."   Is it right to cite Gallio as an illustration
of religious indifference ?   How long did Paul carry on his gospel
work in Corinth (18 : 11; cf. 18 : 18)?   Was the outcome of the work a
large, strong body of believers, some of them Jews but the great
majority Gentiles ?   Study the Corinthian epistles as fully as time permits, to learn of the environment in which the Corinthian church was
founded.   Note that during the early part of Paul's period of work in
Corinth he wrote the two epistles to the Thessalonians.

10. *The return to Antioch and results of the tour.*— In what year,
and at what time of the year, did Paul leave Corinth to return to Antioch
of Syria ?   Where and what was Cenchreæ ?   Are we to understand from
18 : 18 that it was Aquila or Paul who had the vow referred to ?   What
was the nature and purpose of this vow?   What significance has the
incident if the vow was Paul's ?   Was there, in fact, anything in Paul's
principles which would deter him, under favorable circumstances, from
performing a vow (cf. Acts 21 : 20-26; 1 Cor. 9 : 19-23)?   Trace upon
the map Paul's route from Cenchreæ to Ephesus.   Had Paul ever been
at Ephesus before ?   Why did he wish to stop briefly there now ?   When
had he previously purposed to work there, and what had deterred him
from doing so (cf. Acts 16 : 6)?   How was Paul received by the Jews
at Ephesus ?   Why did he not stay longer with them at this time ?
Whither did he go from there ?   Are we to understand from the phrase
(18 : 22) "he went up and saluted the church " that Paul visited Jerusalem before going back to Antioch?   Was this Paul's fourth Christian visit
to Jerusalem (cf. Acts 9 : 26; 11 : 30; 15 : 2)?   What was Paul's purpose
in this visit ?   What did the visit accomplish ?   Why is so slight reference made to it ?   Why did Paul return to Antioch at the close of
this second evangelizing tour ?   Reviewing now the tour as a whole,
what was accomplished in the way of revisitation of churches already
established, and how much time was given to this branch of the work?
How many new churches were founded, and at what places?   How

much time was occupied with the new work? Which of Paul's extant letters were written on this journey? How important for the spread and truth of Christianity was this work which Paul and his fellow-workers were doing?

III. OBSERVATIONS AND TEACHINGS.

1. *Organization.*—No information is given in the Acts or Thessalonian epistles concerning the organization of the Christians which were the result of Paul's labors.—It is to be understood, however, that elders were appointed in each community, according to the custom adopted upon the first tour (*cf.* Acts 14: 23).—When Paul wrote his letter to the Philippians from Rome in 63 A. D. he mentioned in the address "bishops and deacons;" the bishops were the same as the elders, but just when the deacons were first appointed in the church of Philippi, or in any church, cannot be known.—Paul addressed the Christians in Thessalonica as the "church of the Thessalonians" (1 Thess. 1: 1; 2 Thess. 1: 1), so that the term "church" was used at least this early of the local body of believers (*cf.* Acts 15: 41; 16: 5).

2. *Environment.* — Paul uniformly taught first among the Jews of each place, and with some success; then, when they became opposed to him, he turned to the Gentiles with the gospel. — The Jews do not seem to have been numerous in Macedonia and Achaia; only in Thessalonica were they sufficiently strong and intolerant to drive Paul from their city, and later from Berœa. — The first persecution of the Christians by the Romans was at Philippi, but it was against Paul and Silas as being troublesome Jews, not against Christianity as such. — Gallio, when Paul was brought before him by the Jews of Corinth, refused to interfere with Paul's activity, judging it to be not in conflict with the provisions of the Roman law.—Thus Judaism was losing its power against the gospel, and the Roman government was giving it protection.

3. *Institutions.*—Neither in the Acts record of this journey nor in the Thessalonian epistles is there reference to the observance of Sunday or of the Lord's Supper; it may, however, be understood that such observance existed, as the latter certainly, and the former probably, were established before this time.—Baptism is again mentioned in connection with the conversion of the Philippian jailer.—The Jewish custom of performing vows seems to have been observed by Paul in one instance, for some unrecorded reason.

4. *Belief and teaching.*—In presenting the gospel to the Jews Paul argued the Messiahship of Jesus by showing from the Old Testament

prophecies how it was necessary for the Christ to suffer and to rise again from the dead.—The Jews were for the most part not convinced, however; and Paul's converts were chiefly from the Gentiles, especially from those devout ones who were regular attendants upon the synagogue services.—At Athens Paul was spiritually impelled to preach against the polytheism of that city of learning and culture; he presented Christianity in its highest form, teaching that there was but one God, wholly spiritual, made manifest in nature and in revelation as Creator, Sustainer, and Governor of the entire physical and moral universe, of whom all men are sons, and through whom all men are brethren.—But the teaching about Jesus and the resurrection was politely scouted by his Athenian hearers.

5. *Daily life.*—The wise and energetic labors of Paul and his fellow-workers, Silas, Timothy, and Luke, arouse supreme admiration; with such missionaries and such a message Christianity must speedily prevail in the world.—The new Christians showed by their lives the purity, joy, and exaltation of the gospel which they professed (*cf.* 1 Thess. 1 : 10. and elsewhere).

6. *Divine guidance.*—Paul was providentially directed on this tour to take up the gospel work in Macedonia and Achaia, Ephesus and its province being left until a later time.—He was given assurance at Corinth that the work he was doing was God's work, and he would be prospered in it.—Through Paul and his fellow-workers the universal and spiritual religion of Christianity was introduced and essentially established among the Gentile peoples.

Literature.—Upon this section see the commentaries on Acts, especially those of GLOAG, HACKETT, MEYER, and the CAMBRIDGE BIBLE. Also McGIFFERT, History of Christianity in the Apostolic Age, pp. 234-274 ; WEIZSÄCKER, Apostolic Age of the Christian Church, Vol. I, pp. 252-302 ; RAMSAY, St. Paul the Traveler, pp. 178-269 ; Church in the Roman Empire, pp. 73-89 ; NEANDER, Planting and Training of the Christian Church, Vol. I, pp. 168-215 ; FARRAR, Life and Work of St. Paul, chaps. 24-28 ; CONYBEARE AND HOWSON, Life and Epistles of St. Paul, chaps. 8 to 12 ; STIFLER, Introduction to the Book of Acts, sec. xiv ; BIBLE DICTIONARY, articles Aquila, Areopagus, Asia, Athens, Barnabas, Berœa, Bithynia, Cenchræa, Claudius (Cæsar), Corinth, Ephesus, Gallio, Luke, Lydia, Macedonia, Mark, Mysia, Philippi, Priscilla, Prison, Scourging, Silas, Thessalonica, Timothy, Troas.

Acts 18:23—21:16.   55-58 A.D.   Asia Minor, Illyricum, Greece.

I. Study of the Facts.

Let the following subclassification of the material in this section be verified, corrected, or improved :

Par. 1. 18:23,   Revisitation of the Churches of the First Tour.

Par. 2. 18:24-28, The Work of Apollos in Ephesus and Corinth.

Par. 3. 19:1-7,   Paul Gives Christian Baptism to Certain Ephesians.

Par. 4. 19:8-20, Two Years of Ministry and Teaching in Ephesus.

Par. 5. 19:21, 22, Paul's Plans for Future Work.

Par. 6. 19:23-41, Uprising of the Ephesian Tradesmen against Paul.

Par. 7. 20:1-6,   Revisitation of the Churches in Greece.

Par. 8. 20:7-12, Incidents of Paul's Week in Troas.

Par. 9. 20:13-16, Paul Journeys toward Jerusalem.

Par. 10. 20:17-35, Paul's Address to the Ephesian Elders.

Par. 11. 20:36-38, The Departure from Miletus.

Par. 12. 20:1-16, Paul Insists on Going to Jerusalem.

1. Prepare a concise abstract of the material contained in this section, noting the chief facts and recounting them in your own language.

2. Write out a careful paraphrase of Paul's address to the Ephesian elders (20:17-35), reproducing as exactly as possible the thought and spirit of the text.

3. Observe the itinerary of the third evangelizing tour, and the kind of work done: (1) Revisitation in Galatia (the territory of the first tour), occupying perhaps one or two months. (2) New work in Ephesus, occupying between two and three years. (3) Revisitation in Macedonia and Achaia, occupying more than three months. (4) Return from Corinth to Jerusalem, by way of Macedonia, Troas, Miletus, Tyre, and Cæsarea, occupying about two months. (5) The Epistle to the Galatians was probably written from Antioch in the year 54 A. D., some little time before the third evangelizing tour was begun.

(6) Three epistles still extant were written on this journey, First Corinthians in the spring of 57 A. D., from Ephesus; Second Corinthians
in the summer of 57 A. D., from Macedonia; Romans in the spring of
58 A. D., from Corinth. (7) Definite mention is made (1 Cor. 5 : 9) of
a letter not now extant, written to the church at Corinth previous to
our canonical First Corinthians.

II. Topics for Investigation.

1. *Paul's plan for the third evangelizing tour.*—Where was Paul
between the second and third tours? Consider the probability, on the
South-Galatian hypothesis, that the epistle to the Galatians was written
at Antioch in this period. In what year did Paul set out on his third
tour? Was he alone at the beginning? What churches did he first
revisit? What is meant (Acts 18 : 23) by "the region of Galatia and
Phrygia"? What important district did he now intend to evangelize
(Acts 16: 6; 18 : 21)? Trace upon the map Paul's journey from Antioch
of Syria to Ephesus. Was the evangelization of Asia from Ephesus
the main purpose and work of the third tour? Did he also plan
work in Illyricum (Rom. 15 : 19, locate upon the map) and revisitation of the churches in Greece? Was it a part of Paul's plan also
to visit Rome and even territory still farther west (Acts 19 : 21; Rom.
15 : 19, 23)?

2. *Apollos' work in Ephesus and Corinth.*—When did Apollos come
to Ephesus, from where, and why? Is anything known of his career
previous to this time? Ascertain something about the life, education,
and type of Judaism of the Alexandrian Jews. What had been the
character of Apollos' religious and intellectual training? Consider his
two greatest qualifications as a religious teacher, eloquence and learning in the Jewish Scriptures (Acts 18 : 24). How much did he know
about Jesus? Why did he not know the full gospel story? What was
taught him by Aquila and Priscilla? Who were they, and whence had
they their Christian instruction? What did Apollos' readiness to receive
their teaching indicate as to his character? Why did he wish to leave
Ephesus and preach in Achaia? What special work did he do (Acts
18: 27, 28)? Consider his labors and influence in Corinth (1 Cor.
1:12; 2:4; 3:4–10); was his work here among Jews or Gentiles? Was
he personally responsible for the actions of the "Apollos" faction in
the Corinthian church?

3. *Johannine and Christian baptism.*—What was the significance of
this rite as used by John the Baptist (Matt. 3:6; Acts 19:4)? Why had

Jesus received it (Matt. 3:13–16)?   What did John himself say of his baptism as compared with that of the coming Messiah (Matt. 3:11)? Why did John continue baptizing (John 4:1) after Jesus began his work?   If John accepted the Messiahship of Jesus, why did he not become a follower of Jesus (comp. Matt. 3:11–17; John 1:29–34, with Matt. 11:3; Luke 7:19, 20)?   What became of the disciples of John after his death: some became disciples of Jesus, some through lack of information remained undeveloped, and some (later called Sabians) asserted that John was the Messiah, thus antagonizing Christianity. Did Jesus use the symbol of baptism after he began his ministry in Galilee?   Why did the disciples of Christ afterward use this rite (Matt. 28:19)?   Were these "certain disciples" (Acts 19:2) at Ephesus con-verts of Apollos' preaching?   Why did they not know of the giving of the Holy Spirit?   Explain what is meant thereby.   What was the difference between the baptism of John and the baptism "into the name of the Lord Jesus" (Acts 19:5)?   Explain the Holy Spirit man-ifestations of tongue-speaking and prophesying (Acts 19:6, cf. 1 Cor. 14:1–19).

4. *Paul's long ministry in Ephesus.*—Locate Ephesus upon the map and ascertain all you can as to its size, the nationalities of its inhabitants, its political, commercial, and social characteristics, and the kinds and condition of religion and morals found there in Paul's time.   Among what class did Paul work during the first three months in this city?   Had he previously been invited to do so (Acts 18:19–21)?   What results attended his work for the Jews?   How did Jewish opposition to the gos-pel after a time manifest itself?   Did the Jews make Paul trouble during his subsequent period of work in Ephesus (Acts 20:19)?   With reference to this consider the whole address in Acts 20:17–35.   After Paul with-drew from his work among the Jews in the synagogue, where and how did he carry on his gospel teaching?   What was the "school of Tyrannus" (Acts 19:9), why did Paul teach there, and what was the relation, if any, of his work to Tyrannus' work?   Who would gather to receive instruction from Paul at this place—Gentiles or Jews, or both, and in what numbers?   How long did this daily instruction continue? Had Paul previously done any teaching that was so regular, systematic, and prolonged?   What did Paul accomplish by this period of work? Was Christianity spread from Ephesus throughout the province of Asia (Acts 19:10)?

5. *Incidents of the work in Ephesus.*—Explain the nature of the handkerchief and apron cures mentioned in Acts 19:12 (cf. Acts 5:12–

16). What was the divine purpose of these miracles? Explain the incident of the Jewish exorcists recorded in Acts 19 : 13–16 (cf. Acts 8 : 4–24 ; 13 : 4–12). Was this humiliating defeat of the sons of Sceva providentally appointed to overthrow their false work? How did the failure of these Jewish exorcists affect the attitude of the people toward Paul and his teaching? What were these books of the "curious arts" (Acts 19 : 19) which were burned? Explain the significance of this victory of Christianity over paganism.

6. *Paul's plans for future work.*— Consider Paul's plans for future activity as set forth in Acts 19 : 21. What is the meaning of the phrase (Acts 19 : 21) "purposed in the spirit"? Why did he send two of his fellow-workers on ahead into Macedonia? How much longer did he himself stay in Ephesus (cf. 1 Cor. 16 : 8, 9)? Why had Paul been for a long time (Rom. 1 : 13 ; 15 : 23) eager to visit Rome? What district still farther west did he have in mind to evangelize (Rom. 15 : 23, 24, 28)? Whither was he going, however, before he visited Rome and Spain (Acts 19 : 21 ; Rom. 15 : 25)? What were Paul's reasons for going to Jerusalem at this time (Rom. 15 : 25, 28)? Observe that 1 Corinthians was written from Ephesus in the spring of 57 A. D., not long before Paul's departure from Ephesus for the fulfilment of his plans to visit Macedonia, Achaia, Jerusalem, Rome, and Spain. Did this plan provide for the evangelization of the entire western world as then known? Why did Paul choose to spread the gospel in the western rather than in the eastern world? Was the eastern world evangelized in the apostolic age? if so, by whom?

7. *The uprising of the Ephesian tradesmen.*— Consider the close resemblance between this uprising at Ephesus and the previous one at Philippi (Acts 16 : 12, 16–24). Are these the only two instances recorded in Acts where the Gentiles were the instigators of the opposition to Christianity? Did money interests lie at the bottom of both troubles? What business was Demetrius in, and how many were associated with him in the trade? Who used the little "shrines" that were made, and for what purpose? Consider the address of Demetrius to the tradesman (Acts 19 : 25–27) as to its shrewdness and ability. How correct and how effective were his two arguments against Paul, that Christianity was ruining their business, and that the worship of Diana was being overthrown? Why did the populace gather in the theater? Of what nationality were Gaius and Aristarchus, and why were they seized? Why did Paul wish to go before the crowd? Who restrained him from so doing, and why?

What action was taken by the "chief officers" of Asia to protect Paul? Why were they friendly to him? What was the idea of the Jews in having Alexander address the populace? Why would they not hear him? Note carefully the four arguments used by the "town clerk" (Acts 19:35-40) in quieting the disturbance. Was his purpose to defend Christianity, or to restore order? What was the result of this uprising as regarded Christianity in Ephesus and the surrounding country?

8. *Revisitation in Macedonia and Achaia.*— In what year, and at what season of the year, did Paul set out on this portion of his third tour (1 Cor. 16:8)? Was the uprising of the tradesmen a cause or the cause of his leaving Ephesus? At what point in Asia did he stop, and for what reasons (2 Cor. 2:12, 13)? Where did Paul at last find Titus (2 Cor. 7:5, 6)? What places in Macedonia would Paul, of course, revisit at this time? Was it from one of these places, perhaps Philippi, that Paul wrote 2 Corinthians, in the summer of 57 A. D.? Why does the Acts give no account (Acts 20:2, 3) of Paul's work in Macedonia and Achaia on this journey? Was it at this time that Paul went to Illyricum, west and north of Macedonia, and preached the gospel (Rom. 15:19)? How long was Paul's stay in Achaia, probably at Corinth (Acts 20:3; 1 Cor. 16:5, 6)? What was the plot laid against Paul by the Jews there? What change of plans for the journey to Jerusalem was made to thwart this plot? Was it just before Paul left Corinth at this time, early in 58 A. D., that he wrote the epistle to the Romans? Trace upon the map this revisitation journey from Ephesus to Corinth.

9. *Paul's fellow-workers on this tour.*— Did Paul start out from Antioch on his third tour alone (*cf.* Acts 13:2-5; 15:36-40; 18:23)? Read through the material of this section (Acts 18:23—21:16) to see who became his principal companions in the work of this tour. Consider the work of Timothy (Acts 19:22; 20:4; Rom. 16:21; 1 Cor. 4:17; 16:10; 2 Cor. 1:1). Consider the work of Titus (2 Cor. 2:12, 13; 7:5-16; 8:16-24; 12:18). When was Luke with Paul on this journey, as indicated by the "we" passages, Acts 20:5—21:16? Consider the work of Apollos, Aquila, and Priscilla (Acts 18:26-28; 1 Cor. 16:12, 19). Also of Aristarchus, Tychicus, Trophimus, Erastus, Gaius, Sosthenes, and others (*cf.* Acts 19:29; 20:4; 1 Cor. 16:15-17; Rom. 16:21-23). What is thus indicated as to the character and methods of Paul's missionary activities? What as to the progress of the gospel?

10. *The return journey from Corinth to Jerusalem.*—Trace upon the map Paul's journey from Corinth to Jerusalem, by way of Philippi, Troas, Miletus, Tyre, Ptolemais, and Cæsarea. In what year, and at what time of the year, did Paul take this journey, and why? Indicate at what places on this journey stops were made, and what time was spent at each. Why are the details of the latter part of the journey given at such length? Can the approximate number of days consumed in going from Corinth to Jerusalem be ascertained (Acts 20 : 6, 13-15; 21 : 4, 7, 15)? How came Paul to stay a week at Troas? Is the farewell meeting there mentioned to introduce the account of the miracle worked by Paul on that occasion? Recount the accident to Eutychus and his restoration to life. Why is this incident given such prominence? Why did Paul stop at Miletus, when he had not wished to take time to stop at Ephesus (Acts 20 : 16, 17)? How far was Miletus from Ephesus, and in what direction? What was the reason for Paul's haste on this journey (Acts 20 : 16)? Why did he wish to be at Jerusalem on the day of Pentecost? Why is the time of the stay at Cæsarea so indefinitely noted? Was the journey overland from Cæsarea to Jerusalem? What was the distance and the nature of the travel? With whom did they lodge at Jerusalem, and why?

11. *Sunday observance among the primitive Christians.*—With reference to this, consider carefully Acts 20 : 7. Why was this meeting on the first day of the week? What was the purpose of the gathering? For other mention in the New Testament of the first day of the week see 1 Cor. 16 : 22; Rev. 1 : 10. When does Sunday observance by the Christians first become explicitly noted (see Justin Martyr, *Apology I*)? Is the growth of this custom to be explained as a commemoration of Christ's resurrection on the first day of the week, and as the meeting of a need for some day to be observed by the Gentile Christians, who had no Sabbath? If this was the origin of Sunday observance by the Christians, is it probable that the custom began very early, even immediately after the resurrection of Christ? Does the comparative silence of New Testament literature and the earliest patristic writings with reference to Sunday observance determine that there was nothing of this kind in the first century, or can that silence be reasonably explained? What was the nature of the first-century Sunday observance — commemoration and religious worship? Was it not until later that Sunday became specifically a day of rest, after the manner of the Jewish Sabbath? Did the Jewish Christians continue to observe the Sabbath, making Sunday observance an additional Christian feature of

the week ?   Had Christ given any instruction that Sunday should be
observed by his disciples instead of the Sabbath ?   Was it practicable
to observe both days; if not, which would survive among the Christians, who were predominantly Gentiles ?   Was the change from Sabbath to Sunday observance in keeping with Christ's teaching and
practice ?   Was this Sunday observance arranged or enjoined by the
apostles ?   Consider carefully and explain Paul's teaching on the subject (Rom. 14:5; Gal. 4:9–11; Col. 2:16, 17).   Is the Christian
Sunday holier than the other days of the week ?   Does it matter which
day of the week is observed, except for the practical value of unifor-
mity ?   Why have a special religious day ?   In what does its proper
observance consist ?

12. *Paul's address to the Ephesian elders.*—Prepare an analysis of this
address (Acts 20:18–35), for which the following may serve as a suggestion : (1) retrospective portion, vss. 18–21; (2) prospective for Paul,
vss. 22–27 ; (3) prospective for the Ephesian church, vss. 28–31; (4)
parting benediction, vss. 32–35.   Why has the historian given so full
an account of this address ?   Are we to suppose that it is reproduced
verbatim, or that only an abstract is given ?   Consider its contents for
thought and language peculiarly Pauline ?   Investigate, if possible, the
textual and theological problem involved in the phrase (vs. 28) "the
church of God."   Consider the chief points of teaching contained in
Paul's words on this occasion.   What are the characteristics of the
address ?   Compare with previous recorded addresses of Paul (Acts
13, 22, 26).   Whence did Paul obtain the precious saying of Jesus used
at the close of verse 35 ?   Do we find, elsewhere in the New Testament, outside of the gospels, any other quotations of Jesus' utterances ?
Are there extra-biblical sayings of Christ in subsequent Christian writings which may be regarded as authentic ?

13. *Predictions of impending trouble for Paul.*—Had Paul feared when
he left Corinth that his mission to Jerusalem would bring him trouble
(*cf.* Rom. 15:31)?   Had this fear become a definite expectation by the
time that he reached Miletus (*cf.* Acts 20:22, 23)?   What was his attitude toward this dark future (*cf.* Acts 20:24)?   Not knowing the
details of the pending trouble, why did Paul think that he would no
more see the Ephesian Christians (Acts 20:25)?   On the view that
there was a release of Paul in 63 A. D. and a subsequent imprisonment
in 65 A. D., is it not altogether probable that he did visit Ephesus
again (*cf.* Phile. 22; 1 Tim. 1:3; 2 Tim. 4:13, 20), and how then
would his misconception at this time be explained ?   What is the mean-

ing of the phrase (Acts 21:4) "through the spirit"?   How was it that
the Christians of Tyre could "through the spirit" advise Paul not to go
to Jerusalem, when he regarded that as his duty?   Did Philip's daughters
at Cæsarea predict the coming trouble to Paul (Acts 21:9)?   Had
Agabus (*cf.* Acts 11:27, 28) come from Judea for the purpose of giving
Paul this warning (Acts 21:10, 11)?   What was his message?   Did he
advise Paul not to go to Jerusalem?   Consider the impressive symbol-
ism which Agabus used in giving his prediction.   Compare the similar
acts of the Old Testament prophets, 1 Kings 22:11; Isa. 20:3; Jer.
13:5-11; 19:10, 11; 27:2; Ezek. 4:1-3; 5:1-4; and elsewhere.
What was the purpose of warning Paul beforehand of this trouble —
to prevent his going to Jerusalem, or to prepare him for what was to
come?   Why did Paul's companions and friends plead with him not
to go to Jerusalem (*cf.* Matt. 16:21-23)?   What was Paul's reply to
their pleadings (Acts 21:13, 14)?   Was it in fact Paul's duty to go?
if so, why?

III.   Observations and Teachings.

1.   *Organization.*—No mention is made in the history or the literature
of the third missionary journey of the Christian organization, aside
from the fact that the elders of the Ephesian church are referred to.—
Deacons are not spoken of, though there may have been such officers.
—The Ephesian elders (or presbyters) were also called bishops (Acts
20:17, 28), which indicates that these three names were used of the
same office in the churches at this time.—The term "church" is commonly employed to denote the local body of believers in any place, so
that the plural form of the word is frequent, *e. g.,* Rom. 16:4, 16;
1 Cor. 7:17; 11:16; 14:33, 34; 16:1, 19; Gal. 1:2, 22.— But
"church" is also used in the singular, though less frequently, to denote
the whole body of Christian believers everywhere, *e. g.,* Acts 9:31; 20:
28; 1 Cor. 10:32; 15:9; Gal. 1:13.

2.   *Environment.*—The Ephesian Jews were comparatively tolerant,
and Paul worked longer among them than was his usual experience,
but they became his bitter enemies and persecutors.—The gospel successfully overcame the Jewish exorcism and heathen magic which had
had a firm hold in Ephesus.— Only twice in Paul's recorded experience did opposition to him originate with the Gentiles; once at
Philippi on the second tour, and once at Ephesus on this third tour;
the cause in both cases was the financial loss brought upon certain
persons through the spread of the gospel.— But at Ephesus Paul was

befriended and protected from the populace by the political officers of the Roman province.

3. *Institutions.*— From the meeting at Troas on the first day of the week and from the reference in 1 Cor. 16:2, it may be inferred that Sunday was at this time observed by the Christians as their especial day of worship, commemorative of Christ's resurrection on that day. —The Sabbath, however, continued to be observed in addition by the Jewish Christians in the Jewish way, this being a part of their former religious life which they had not yet outgrown.—The "breaking of bread" at Troas is to be understood as meaning the Lord's Supper; and extended reference is also made to this rite in 1 Cor. 11:17-34.— The baptism into the name of Jesus was contrasted with the baptism of John, which was a preparatory rite, a pledge of repentance, and a symbol of initiation into the kingdom of the Messiah of God; while Christian baptism was an acknowledgment of, belief in, and self-committal to Jesus Christ, which acknowledgment seems to have been attended in the apostolic era with the bestowal of the extraordinary gifts of tongue-speaking and prophesying.

4. *Belief and teaching.*—The only address or sermon of Paul recorded on this tour was that to the Ephesian elders, in which he directed their attention to the faithful, lowly, and successful ministry which he had served among them (Acts 20:19-21, 26, 27, 31, 33-35), and exhorted them to continue in his footsteps.—The epistles which Paul wrote upon this tour are his greatest, and contain the main body of his teaching as it has come down to us.

5. *Daily life.*— Paul had a large number of fellow-workers with him at various points in his tour; some were Gentiles, some were Hellenists; the most prominent among them were Timothy and Titus.—Apollos, who was a learned and eloquent Jew from Alexandria, became a most efficient Christian evangelist.— In Ephesus Paul gave daily instruction in the gospel for two years, a more systematic period of teaching than is recorded of him elsewhere.— In Paul's epistles to the Corinthians we see portrayed much of the daily life of one of Paul's greatest churches, a life by no means ideal or perfect, and yet reflecting the glory, exaltation, and power of the Christian religion.

6. *Divine guidance.*— Paul's third evangelizing tour was in the main a long period of work in Asia at Ephesus, where he had desired to labor on the second tour, but had then been providentially directed into Macedonia.— By his work at Ephesus he had established the gos-

pel widely and permanently in the whole province of Asia.— Paul's divinely inspired purpose embraced the entire evangelization of the civilized world west of Palestine, including Greece, Italy, and Spain.— Paul went to Jerusalem in 58 A. D. under the leading of the Spirit, conscious of and prepared for the impending trouble, setting aside the protests of his friends and advisers.

Literature.— Upon this section see the commentaries on Acts, especially those of GLOAG, HACKETT, MEYER, and the CAMBRIDGE BIBLE. Also McGIFFERT, History of Christianity in the Apostolic Age, pp. 275–337; WEIZSÄCKER, Apostolic Age of the Christian Church, Vol. I, pp. 303–405; RAMSAY, St. Paul the Traveler, pp. 269–303; Church in the Roman Empire, pp. 90–168; NEANDER, Planting and Training of the Christian Church, Vol. I, pp. 215–301; FARRAR, Life and Work of St. Paul, chaps. 31 to 40a; CONYBEARE AND HOWSON, Life and Epistles of St. Paul, chaps. 13 to 20; STIFLER, Introduction to the Book of Acts, secs. xv, xvi; BIBLE DICTIONARY, articles Agabus, Alexander, Alexandria, Apollos, Aquila, Aristarchus, Artemis, Asiarchs, Baptism, Demetrius, Ephesus, Eutychus, Exorcism, John (the Baptist), Luke, Magic, Priscilla, Rome, Timothy, Titus, Troas, Trophimus, Tychicus, Tyrannus.

Sec. 20.   PAUL'S ARREST AT JERUSALEM THROUGH
JEWISH ENMITY.

Acts 21 : 17— 22 : 29.   58 A. D.   Jerusalem.

I. Study of the Facts.

Let the following subclassification of the material in this section be
verified, corrected, or improved :

Par. 1. 21 : 17–26, Paul's Effort to Conciliate the Jewish Christians.

Par. 2. 21 : 27–30, Assault of the Jews upon Paul in Jerusalem.

Par. 3. 21 : 31–40, Paul Rescued and Protected by the Roman Soldiers.

Par. 4. 22 : 1–21, Paul's Apologetic Address to his Jewish Enemies.

Par. 5. 22 : 22–29, Paul's Prerogatives as a Roman Citizen.

1. Prepare a concise abstract of the material contained in this section, noting the chief facts and recounting them in your own language.

2. Write out a careful paraphrase of Paul's address to the Jews
(22 : 1–21), reproducing as exactly as possible the apostle's thought and
spirit.

II. Topics for Investigation.

1. *Paul's fifth Christian visit to Jerusalem.*— For the previous four
visits confer Acts 9 : 26 (Gal. 1 : 18); 11 : 30; 15 : 4 (Gal. 2 : 1); 18 : 22.
In what year and at what season of the year (Acts 20 : 16) was this
fifth visit to Jerusalem ? What primary purpose (Rom. 15 : 28), and
what secondary purposes, had Paul in making this visit ? Why did Paul
stay while in the city with Mnason, a Hellenist Jew from Cyprus (Acts
21 : 16) ? Who are meant by "the brethren" (21 : 17), Mnason and his
friends, or the Jewish Christians of Jerusalem generally? Who is the
"James" referred to in 21 : 18 ? Why is no mention made of Peter,
John, or any others of the original twelve apostles ? How was Paul
received by James and the leaders of the Jerusalem church ? What was
the feeling toward Paul of the Jewish Christians as a body in Jerusalem ? On the term "thousands" (21 : 20) see R. V. marg. rdg., which
represents the Greek. What is the meaning of 21 : 20, last clause ?
How could the Jerusalem Christians so distrust Paul, in view of the

decision of the Jerusalem Conference seven years before (Acts 15 ; Gal.
2 : 1–10) ?   Had Paul in fact done what they (21 : 21) had heard
reported of him (*cf.* 1 Cor. 7 : 18–20) ?

2. *Paul's conference with the leaders of the Jerusalem church.*— How
soon after Paul's arrival in the city did he confer with the church
leaders ?   Was the meeting a formal one ?   Was it a meeting of the
church officers only, or of all the Christians ?   What position had
these men taken (Acts 15 ; Gal. 2 : 1–10) regarding Paul and his
work ?   Had Paul been at Jerusalem again since that time (*cf.* Acts
18 : 22), and, if so, what had been done ?   What part did Paul take in
this meeting on the fifth visit ?   State what information he could give
them as to the work of his third missionary journey.   How was his
report received ?   Why is no mention made here in Acts of the
collection which Paul had brought, as the chief purpose of his visit,
from the Gentile Christians to the Jewish Christians ?   What action
was recommended to Paul by the Jerusalem leaders ?   For what
reason ?   Was the recommendation a wise and reasonable one ?   How
large was the class of Jewish Christians on behalf of whom this course
was taken ?   Would the performance of it indeed remove their suspicion of Paul ?

3. *Paul's participation in the Nazaritic vow.*—What was the nature
and purpose of the Nazaritic vow (*cf.* Num. 6 : 1–21) ?   Was this in
fact an instance of it ?   Describe the details of the performance of this
vow.   Is it to be understood that the four men with whom Paul associated himself in its observance were Jewish Christians ?   Did the recommendation of the Jewish leaders contemplate a complete performance
of the vow by Paul, or only a partial participation of Paul in the vow
of the four men (21 : 24) ?   In the case of mere participation, what
would have fallen to Paul to do (21 : 24, 26) ?   Was Paul's performance
of, or participation in, this vow inconsistent either with his principles
or with his practice (*cf.* 1 Cor. 9 : 19–23 ; Rom. 14 : 1, 2) ?   Explain
Paul's attitude toward external Judaism as regards principle and practice (*a*) for himself, (*b*) for Jewish Christians, (*c*) for Gentile Christians.   Did the observance of this vow by Paul accomplish what was
intended — did the Jewish Christians, because of it, put confidence in,
and extend complete fellowship to, Paul ?

4. *The assault of the Jews upon Paul.*—What was the feeling of the
non-Christian Jews in Jerusalem toward Paul ?   What had Paul feared
concerning this visit to the city (*cf.* Acts 20 : 22–24 ; 21 : 10–14 ; Rom.
15 : 31) ?   Who instigated the attack upon Paul (21 : 27) ?   How came

they to be in Jerusalem?   Why did they hate the apostle (*cf.* Acts
20 : 19)?   Why were the Jerusalem Jews ready to join in the assault?
What charges did they bring against Paul (21 : 28, 29)?   Were these
charges true?   Had Paul in fact, in his general teaching, denounced
the Jewish nation, the Mosaic system, and the temple at Jerusalem?
Had Paul in fact taken Trophimus, a Greek, into the portion of the
temple permitted only to the Jews?   Would he refrain from doing so
on the ground of principle or of expediency?   Were the charges seri-
ously believed by the Jews, or were they rather an excuse for the vent-
ing of their hatred toward him?   Would they have killed him if he
had not been taken out of their hands?   By whom was he rescued, and
how?   Whither was Paul taken, and for what purpose?   Did the
Roman captain attempt to get at the facts in the case?   Whom did he
at first suppose Paul to be, and why?   What is known about the
Egyptian and the assassins here referred to (21 : 38)?   What immunity
and respect did Paul secure for himself by making known his Roman
citizenship?

   5. *Paul's address to the Jewish mob.*— For what did the mob who had
assaulted him clamor (21 : 36; *cf.* 22 : 22; 25 : 24; Luke 23 : 18)?   Why
did Paul wish to address his enemies?   Why did he speak to them in
the "Hebrew" (*i. e.*, Aramaic) language?   Explain the terms "brethren
and fathers" (22 : 1).   Was it Paul's purpose in this speech to reply
directly to the charge that he was everywhere teaching against Judaism?   Prepare an analysis of Paul's defense, for which the following
may give suggestion: (1) introduction, vss. 1, 2; (2) he had been a
strict Jew like themselves, vss. 3–5, (3) until God had shown him the
truth of the gospel, vss. 6–16, (4) and had appointed him to a Gentile
ministry, vss. 17–21.   Observe carefully the facts stated here as to
Paul's early life.   Make a detailed study of this account, by Paul himself, of his conversion, comparing with it the previous account in
9 : 1–19.   Consider the divine revelation here recorded (22 : 17–21), as
to when it took place, why it is not mentioned in its chronological
position in Acts, why no mention of it is made at all in Gal. 1 : 17, 18,
and what the purpose of the revelation was.   What features of the address
were calculated to have a soothing and winning effect upon his hearers?   Characterize the address as to the ability, wisdom, and sincerity
of Paul manifested in it?   How was the account of this address
obtained for the book of Acts?   What was the effect of the address
upon his Jewish enemies?   Was he allowed to finish what he wished
to say (22 : 22)?

III. Observations and Teachings.

These concluding chapters of Acts (chaps. 21–28) deal exclusively with the arrest, trials, and imprisonments of Paul. For that reason they contribute almost no information concerning the main topics of the general history of Christianity in this period, their organization, institutions, environment, belief and teaching, daily life, and divine guidance. There are, however, observations to be made upon this portion of the history, and teachings to be drawn from it. The student will make note of such as seem to him deserving of special mention.

Literature.— Upon this section see the commentaries on Acts, especially those of GLOAG, HACKETT, MEYER, and the CAMBRIDGE BIBLE. Also McGIFFERT, History of Christianity in the Apostolic Age, pp. 338–350 ; WEIZSÄCKER, Apostolic Age of the Christian Church, Vol. II, pp. 13–15; NEANDER, Planting and Training of the Christian Church, Vol. I, pp. 301–306; FARRAR, Life and Work of St. Paul, chap. 40; CONYBEARE AND HOWSON, Life and Epistles of St. Paul, chap. 21; STIFLER, Introduction to the Book of Acts, sec. xvii; BIBLE DICTIONARY, articles Ananias, Antonia, Damascus, Elder, Hebrew Language, James, Paul, Romans, Roman Citizenship, Tarsus, Temple, Trophimus, Vows.

SEC. 21. TRIAL OF PAUL BEFORE THE SANHEDRIN.

Acts 22 : 30 — 23 : 35.   58 A. D.   Jerusalem.

I. STUDY OF THE FACTS.

Let the following subclassification of the material in this section be verified, corrected, or improved :

Par. 1. 22 : 30—23 : 10, The Trial of Paul before the Sanhedrin.

Par. 2. 23 : 11,   Paul Divinely Assured of a Ministry in Rome.

Par. 3. 23 : 12–15, The Conspiracy of the Jews against Paul.

Par. 4. 23 : 16–22, The Plot Made Known to the Roman Officials.

Par. 5. 23 : 23–35, Paul Removed for Safety to Cæsarea.

Prepare a careful abstract of the material contained in this section.

II. TOPICS FOR INVESTIGATION.

1. *The attempted examination of Paul before the Sanhedrin.*—What authority had the Romans at this time over the assemblage and the acts of the Jewish Sanhedrin ? By whom was the Sanhedrin on this occasion called together? For what purpose (22 : 30) ? With what statement did Paul begin his defense of himself ? Why did Paul address the Sanhedrists as "brethren" ? With vs. 1, last clause, compare Acts 24 : 16 ; 2 Tim. 1 : 3. In view of the Jewish charges against him, what did Paul mean by his claim that he had up to this time lived in all good conscience before God ? Why was the high priest greatly incensed at these words of the apostle ? How did he resent them, and why ? What reply did Paul make ? Explain the phrase "whited wall" (vs. 3, *cf.* Matt. 23 : 27). What apology did the apostle subsequently make (vs. 5) for his rebuke of Ananias, and on what grounds ? What did he mean by saying "I wist not that he was high priest" ? What is known about the high priest Ananias ? Explain the oriental custom of smiting referred to in vs. 2.

2. *The stratagem of Paul at the trial.*—Was it apparent, from the reception given Paul's first words, that a fair trial could not be had ? Instead of attempting to continue his defense, what did Paul do ? What did he hope to gain by raising this issue among the Sanhedrists ? Was it honest and worthy of the apostle to resort to this stratagem in self-defense ? Which of the two parties predominated in numbers in the Sanhedrin, and which in official power ? What were the reasons

for the difference and hostility between the two parties ?   With which party did Paul emphatically ally himself, and why (*cf.* Acts 22 : 3 ; 26 : 5 ; Phil. 3 : 5) ?   Explain the phrase (vs. 6) "the hope and resurrection of the dead."   How was it concerning this that Paul was on trial ?   What attitude did the Pharisaic party then assume toward Paul ?   What was the motive of their action ; sympathy with Christianity, or a desire to make a point against the Sadducees ?   Compare with this incident that recorded in Acts 5 : 27–40.   What was the outcome of this dissension stirred up by Paul ?   How was he rescued from the hands of his enemies ?

3. *Comparison with the trials of Jesus and Stephen.*—Make a careful review of the trial of Jesus (Luke 23 : 1–24, and parallel accounts in Matt. and Mark ; John 18 : 19–24, 28–40) ; also of the trial of Stephen (Acts 6 : 8—7 : 57).   Who were the leaders of the persecution in the case of Jesus, Stephen, and Paul, respectively ?   What charge was brought against the accused in each case, and how was it presented ? What was the defense of each one ?   Were there violence, irregularity, and injustice, in all three trials ?   What was the outcome of each trial, and why ?   Were the Jews, as represented by their national leaders, any nearer to an acceptance of Christianity in 58 A. D. than they were in 30 or in 33 A. D.?

4. *Paul's future ministry in Rome.*—Consider the time, manner, and purpose of the divine assurance given Paul that he was still to work in Rome.   Describe Paul's previous hopes and plans for visiting Rome (Acts 19 : 21 ; Rom. 1 : 11–13 ; 15 : 22–32, and elsewhere). Did Paul need such encouragement to sustain him in the long imprisonment upon which he was entering ?   Why was it necessary (vs. 11) that Paul should preach the gospel in Rome ?   Consider the providential guidance of Paul at previous crises (Acts 9 : 1–19 ; 16 : 6–10 ; 22 : 17–21, and elsewhere).

5. *The plot of the Jews against Paul.*—Describe the plot which was laid by the Jews to assassinate Paul.   How many, and who, were the Jews engaged in this conspiracy ?   How did any of the Sanhedrists dare to join in so illegal, secret, and violent a plot ?   Could they religiously justify themselves in the undertaking ?   Compare these plotting Jews with those who crucified Christ, and with those who, stoned Stephen.   Why did they not put Paul to death as they had done with them ?   Consider other instances in which Paul was protected by the Roman government from his enemies.   Would the Jewish plot probably have succeeded except for the fortunate and timely discovery of

it by Paul's nephew ?   Is anything further known about him, or about
any of Paul's immediate relatives ?   How was the matter made known
to the Roman authorities ?   Had the Romans no power or disposition
to punish such conspirators as these ?

6. *The removal of Paul to Cæsarea.*—What did Lysias do with Paul
to protect him from the Jewish plot ?   Why was Cæsarea chosen as the
place (vss. 24, 33) ?   Was the action of the Roman captain in this
whole matter faithful to duty and commendable ?   What escort did he
provide for Paul on this journey ?   Why so large a body of soldiers ?
Locate Cæsarea upon the map.   Ascertain as well as you can the time
and circumstances incident to a journey thither from Jerusalem.   To
whom was Paul delivered in Cæsarea, and why ?   How did Lysias
communicate to Felix the facts in this case (vss. 25-30) ?   Did the
letter contain an exact statement of the facts (see especially vs. 27, last
clause ; compare Acts 21 : 31-40 ; 22 : 25-29) ?   How came this letter
to be preserved, and to find its way into the book of Acts ?   With vs.
29 compare Acts 18 : 12-17 ; 25 : 17-21.   What had the trial before
the Sanhedrin disclosed as to whether Paul was innocent or guilty ?
Why had not Lysias therefore released Paul, or had he power only to
refer the case ?   What disposition of the case did Felix temporarily
make ?   Where was Paul kept in custody until he could be formally
tried ?

III. OBSERVATIONS AND TEACHINGS.

For directions as to the work to be done under this head, see the statement at this point in Sec. 20.

Literature.—Upon this section see the commentaries on Acts, especially those of
GLOAG, HACKETT, MEYER, and the CAMBRIDGE BIBLE.   Also McGIFFERT, History of Christianity in the Apostolic Age, pp. 350, 351 ; NEANDER, Planting and
Training of the Christian Church, Vol. I, pp. 306-308 ; FARRAR, Life and Work
of St. Paul, chap. 40 ; CONYBEARE AND HOWSON, Life and Epistles of St. Paul, chap.
21 ; STIFLER, Introduction to the Book of Acts, sec. xvii ; BIBLE DICTIONARY,
articles Ananias, Antipatris, Cæsarea, Claudius Lysias, Felix, High Priest, Paul,
Pharisees, Sadducees. Sanhedrin.

Acts 24 : 1—25 : 12.   58-60 A. D.   Cæsarea.

I. STUDY OF THE FACTS.

Let the following subclassification of the material in this section be verified, corrected, or improved :

Par. 1. 24 : 1–9,   The Trial before Felix — the Prosecution.

Par. 2. 24 : 10–21,   The Trial before Felix — Paul's Defense.

Par. 3. 24 : 22–26,   Action upon the Case Deferred by Felix.

Par. 4. 24 : 27—25 : 5, Festus, Felix's Successor, Importuned against Paul.

Par. 5. 25 : 6–12,   The Trial before Festus and Appeal to Cæsar.

1. Prepare a careful abstract of the material contained in this section.

2. Write out a paraphrase, reproducing as exactly as possible, in your own language, the thought and spirit of the original, (*a*) of Tertullus' address (24 : 2–8), (*b*) of Paul's address (24 : 10–21).

II. TOPICS FOR INVESTIGATION.

1. *Tertullus' speech in accusation of Paul.*— How long a time intervened between the Sanhedrin trial of Paul (23 : 1–10) and this hearing before Felix? Who came to Cæsarea to prosecute the case against Paul? Who was Tertullus? Why did the Jews employ him to represent them in the trial? Prepare an analysis of Tertullus' speech, for which the following may afford suggestion : (1) the exordium, vss. 2*b*–4 ; (2) three distinct charges against Paul : sedition, heresy, sacrilege, vss. 5, 6 ; (3) the peroration, vs. 8. Is this probably a mere outline of what was said? Was Felix deserving of the praise bestowed upon him (vss. 2, 3)? With "mover of insurrections" (vs. 5) compare Acts 16 : 20 ; 17 : 6 ; 21 : 28 ; Luke 23 : 2. Explain the title "Nazarenes" (vs. 5 ; Matt. 2 : 23 ; Mark 14 : 67 ; 16 : 6). With vs. 6 compare Acts 21 : 28, 29. Consider in detail the three charges against Paul, as to the meaning, basis, and reason for each. Who (vs. 9) arranged and supported theses charges against the apostle? What was the object of Tertullus : (*a*) to get from Felix a condemnation of Paul ; or (*b*) to persuade Felix to remand the case to the Sanhedrin (*cf.* Acts 25 : 3, 15, 16)?

2. *The defense of Paul before Felix.*— Why did the apostle present his own defense, instead of making it through an advocate, as did the Jews? What were Paul's qualifications as a jurist and advocate? Have we anything more than an outline of his address? Was Luke present at the trials of Paul (*cf.* Acts 21 : 17 ; 27 : 1)? If so, was he probably himself the source of these accounts of the trials? Prepare an analysis of Paul s address, for which the following may afford suggestion : (1) introduction, vs. 10 ; (2) reply to each of the charges: sedition, vss. 11, 12 ; heresy, vss. 14–16 ; sacrilege, vss. 17, 18 ; (3) demand for a fair trial, vss. 19–21. Consider the simple but skillful preface to Paul's defense. How did Felix's long official career promise well for Paul? Why did Paul call attention (vs. 11) to the fact that he had not yet been in Palestine two weeks? Consider carefully Paul's reply to the charge of sedition (vss. 12, 13). What defense did he make against the accusation of heresy (vss. 14–16)? Explain the term "the way" (vs. 14 ; *cf.* 22 : 4 ; 24 : 22, and elsewhere). What is the meaning of "a sect" (vs. 14)? With vs. 16 compare Acts 23 : 1. How could Paul claim to be loyal to Judaism, in view of his gospel beliefs and work? Acknowledging that he was the leader of the gospel sect, did he claim for it the same immunity that was accorded to other Jewish sects? Consider carefully Paul's reply to the charge of sacrilege (vss. 17, 18). Observe in vs. 17 the only reference in Acts to the Pauline collection (*cf.* Rom. 15 : 25, 26, and elsewhere). Had Paul in fact taken a Gentile into the portion of the temple allowed only to Jews (*cf.* Acts 21 : 27)? With vs. 21 compare vs. 15 ; 23 : 6–9. What irregularity in the trial against him did Paul point out (vss. 18–20) and demand rectification of?

3. *Felix and his attitude toward the case.*— Ascertain all that can be known about Felix. What is meant (vs. 22*a*) by the statement that Felix had "more exact knowledge concerning the way"? What were the reasons why Felix put off a decision in Paul's case (vss. 22, 26)? How could Felix suppose that either Paul or his friends would buy his freedom? On Paul's ability to meet the expenses of his trials see Ramsay, *St. Paul the Traveler*, pp. 310–312. How long was the decision deferred (vs. 27)? Explain Paul's relations with Felix during this interval (vss. 24–26). What were the features of Paul's imprisonment at this time (vs. 23)? Could he carry on his missionary work in any way during this period? What was the divine purpose of Paul's long imprisonment in Cæsarea? What terminated Felix's relation to Paul and his case?

4. *The trial of Paul before Festus.*—Ascertain all that can be known about Festus. In what year, and why, did he succeed Felix as the governor of the Roman province of Judea? Why did the Roman governor make his headquarters at Cæsarea? How soon after his arrival in the province was Paul's case brought before Festus? By whom, where, and why? Did they desire from Festus a condemnation of the apostle, or the transfer of his trial to Jerusalem (*cf.* 25 : 3, 15, 16 ; 23 : 12-21)? Explain this persistent Jewish hatred. Observe Festus' honest, dignified, and judicial treatment of the matter. When did Paul have a hearing before Festus? Consider that this trial is the third in the series (before the Sanhedrin, before Felix, before Festus), and the last before his Roman trials. What charges were brought against Paul in the trial before Festus (*cf.* vs. 8, presumably the same as in the former trial, 24 : 5)? What was Paul's reply to these accusations? Why does not the Acts contain an account of these speeches? What did Festus decide as to Paul's innocence or guilt relative to the Roman law (*cf.* Acts 25 : 18-20 ; 18 : 12-17)? What question did he put to Paul (vs. 9), and why? Why did not Festus acquit Paul? Compare Festus with Felix in their relation to Paul.

5. *The appeal to Rome.*—How did Paul remove his case from both Festus and the Jews? Describe the right of a Roman citizen to appeal his case from the provincial court to the imperial tribunal at Rome. Upon what conditions only was such an appeal granted? What was "the council" (vs. 12), and why did Festus confer with these councillors? What led Paul to make the appeal : (*a*) the belief that he would not obtain justice or release in Judea (but *cf.* Acts 26 : 32); (*b*) the knowledge that he was divinely appointed (Acts 23 : 11) to go to Rome? What did Paul anticipate would be the outcome of his case in the Roman courts?

III. OBSERVATIONS AND TEACHINGS.

For directions as to the work to be done under this head, see the statement at this point in Sec. 20.

Literature.—Upon this section see the commentaries on Acts, especially those of GLOAG, HACKETT, MEYER, and the CAMBRIDGE BIBLE. Also McGIFFERT, History of Christianity in the Apostolic Age, pp. 351-355 ; RAMSAY, St. Paul the Traveler, pp. 303-313; NEANDER, Planting and Training of the Christian Church, Vol. 1, pp. 308, 309 ; FARRAR, Life and Work of St. Paul, chap. 41 ; CONYBEARE AND HOWSON, Life and Epistles of St. Paul, chap. 22 ; STIFLER, Introduction to the Book of Acts, sec. xviii ; BIBLE DICTIONARY, articles Ananias, Cæsar, Cæsarea, Drusilla, Felix, Festus, Lysias, Nazarenes, Paul, Tertullus.

SEC. 23. PAUL'S HEARING BEFORE AGRIPPA.

Acts 25 : 13 — 26 : 32. 60 A. D. Cæsarea.

I. STUDY OF THE FACTS.

Let the following subclassification of the material in this section be verified, corrected, or improved:

Par. 1. 25 : 13–22, The Consultation of Festus with Agrippa concerning Paul.

Par. 2. 25 : 23–27, The Examination, Festus' statement of the case.

Par. 3. 26 : 1–23, The Examination, Paul's Defense.

Par. 4. 26 : 24–29, Interruption and Conclusion of the Defense.

Par. 5. 26 : 30–32, Agrippa's Declaration of the Innocence of Paul.

1. Prepare a concise abstract of the material contained in this section, noting the chief facts and recounting them in your own language.

2. Write out a careful paraphrase of Paul's defense before Agrippa (26 : 1–23), reproducing in words of your own the thought and spirit of the apostle.

II. TOPICS FOR INVESTIGATION.

1. *Festus' consultation with Agrippa about Paul.*—Which Agrippa was this? Ascertain what is known about him. Over what territory was he the ruler? Investigate the relationships between Agrippa, Bernice, Drusilla and Felix (*cf.* Acts 24 : 24 ; 25 : 3). What was the official relation of the Jewish king Agrippa to the Roman procurator Festus? For what purpose did Agrippa come to Cæsarea in 60 A. D.? Why did Festus wish to consult with him concerning Paul? When did this hearing take place? Consider carefully Festus' presentation of the case to Agrippa (25 : 14–21). Compare with this the previous Acts account of the matter (25 : 1–12). Had Festus naturally supposed that Paul was guilty of some crime under the Roman law? What had the trial, however, shown to be the case (*cf.* 25 : 18, 19)? What were the religious questions about which the Jews had accused the apostle? Was Festus interested in these, or capable of passing upon them (*cf.* Acts 18 : 12–17)? Why did he nevertheless feel a duty regarding the Jewish complaint? For what reason did he propose to Paul that his case be transferred to Jerusalem (25 : 20, *cf.* 25 : 9)? Did Paul's appeal

to Cæsar take his case out of Festus' hands? Of what importance
then was Agrippa's opinion about Paul? Had Festus the duty of sending with Paul to Rome a statement of his case, which statement he
wished to have as accurate as possible (25 : 25, 27)? Investigate this
Roman custom of *litteræ dimissoriæ.* Would Agrippa, because he was
a Jew (26 : 2, 3), be able to advise Festus concerning the religious
accusations of the Jews against Paul? Who were assembled with the
governor and the king to hear Paul's defense, and why? Who presided at this examination? Picture to yourself, as graphically and
accurately as may be, the scene depicted in 25 : 23. Consider the preliminary statement of the case made to the assembly by Festus (25 : 24
–27) containing three points: (1) the accusation of Paul by the Jews,
(2) his own judgment of Paul's innocence under Roman law, (3) the
particular reason for this examination.

2. *Paul's apology before Agrippa.*— Prepare a careful analysis of this
speech of the apostle (26 : 1–23), for which the following outline may
give suggestion: (1) introduction, vss. 2, 3; (2) his loyalty to strict
Judaism in his early religion and career, vss. 4–11; (3) his conversion
and its results, by which he was divinely led to accept and to preach
the gospel, vss. 12–20; (4) his present position persecuted for advocat-
ing Christianity as the true fulfilment of Judaism, vss. 21–23. Was the
address interrupted by Festus at this point (25 : 23), or had Paul com-
pleted what he wished to say? Compare this speech in detail with
that given by Paul from the castle steps (Acts 22 : 1–21), as to whether
both contain in general the same material, have the same point, and
present the same argument. What matter is peculiar to this account
of chap. 26? How did this defense before Agrippa differ from the
apologetic speeches in the two trials before Felix and Festus (24 : 10–
21; 25 : 8). Why the difference? Explain Paul's interpretation of
the Messianic hope of Israel (26 : 6–8), Consider carefully the meaning of 26 : 9, *cf.* 1 Tim. 1 : 13; John 16 : 2. What two interpretations
are given of 26 : 10, last clause, and which is to be accepted? Compare this account of Paul's conversion with those in chaps. 9 and 22.
In the matter of the commission of Jesus to Paul (26 : 16–18) explain
how it comes that the substance of the divine revelations made to Pau.
at different and subsequent times (if the other accounts are correct) are
here fused together, and put directly into the mouth of Jesus at the
Damascus revelation. Compare 26 : 20 with Gal. 1 : 18–24. On 26 : 23
see Isa. 9 : 2; 42 : 16; 49 : 6; 60 : 2. Describe from 26 : 22, 23 Paul's
attitude as a Christian toward Judaism. Consider the source and the

historical trustworthiness of this account of the apostle's speech before Agrippa.   What are the chief characteristics of this address ?

3. *Paul's concluding words and Agrippa's decision.*— Explain Festus' impatient complaint against Paul, and consider Paul's sincere and informing reply (26 : 24–26).   Were Paul's words incomprehensible to Festus because of the latter's Roman ignorance of the Jewish history and religion, his insusceptibility to high spiritual conceptions and truth, and his dislike of enthusiasm ?   Was Paul understood by Agrippa, to whom primarily he had been speaking ?   What was the purpose of Paul's appeal to Agrippa in 26 : 27 ?   Consider carefully the meaning of Agrippa's reply (26 : 28), comparing the translations of AV and RV, and judging which interpretation gives the truer view of the situation and of the Jewish king.   Who conferred together at the close of this hearing of Paul, and for what purpose ?   What was the general opinion expressed concerning the case (26 : 31)?   What was Agrippa's decision (26 : 32) concerning Paul's innocence or guilt relative to the Jewish charges against him ?   Would Paul's Jewish accusers have considered Agrippa a sufficiently loyal and strict Jew to be qualified to pass an acceptable opinion on Paul's relation to Judaism ?   If Paul might have been released, had not the appeal to Rome been taken, as Agrippa judged, then was the appeal a mistake on Paul's part ?   Would Festus' report of the case to the imperial tribunal at Rome be such as quite certainly to secure Paul's acquittal ?

III. Observations and Teachings.

For directions as to the work to be done under this head, see the statement at this point in Sec. 20.

Literature.— Upon this section see the commentaries on Acts, especially those of Gloag, Hackett, Meyer, and the Cambridge Bible.   Also McGiffert, History of Christianity in the Apostolic Age, pp. 355, 356; Neander, Planting and Training of the Christian Church, Vol. I, pp. 309–311; Farrar, Life and Work of St. Paul, chap. 42; Conybeare and Howson, Life and Epistles of St. Paul, chap. 22; Stifler, Introduction to the Book of Acts, sec. xviii; Bible Dictionary, articles Agrippa, Appeal, Bernice, Cæsar, Cæsarea, Festus, Paul.

Sec. 24. TRANSFER TO AND IMPRISONMENT AT ROME.

Acts 27 : 1—28 : 31.   60-63 A.D.   Cæsarea, Malta, Rome.

I. Study of the Facts.

Let the following subclassification of the material in this section be verified, corrected, or improved:

Par. 1. 27 : 1–8,   Beginning of the Voyage to Italy.

Par. 2. 27 : 9–44,   The Shipwreck on the Way.

Par. 3. 28 : 1–10,   Incidents of the Winter Stay in Malta.

Par. 4. 28 : 11–16, End of the Journey, and Arrival in Rome.

Par. 5. 28 : 17–22, Paul's First Conference with the Jews at Rome.

Par. 6. 28 : 23–28, Paul's Second Conference with the Jews at Rome.

Par. 7. 28 : 30, 31, Paul's Circumstances and Work during the Long Captivity.

1. Prepare an abstract of the material contained in this section.

2. Prepare a concise paraphrase of Paul's addresses to the Jews (28 : 17–28), reproducing as exactly as possible the apostle's thought and spirit.

II. Topics for Investigation.

1. *The voyage from Cæsarea to Malta.*— In what year, and at what season of the year, was Paul sent a prisoner to Rome? How long was this after his final trial before Festus and his appeal to Cæsar? Who were Paul's Christian companions on this journey to Rome? Who was in charge of Paul as a Roman prisoner? Were there also other prisoners besides himself in the party? How was Paul treated (Acts 27 : 3), and why? Did they go on a ship bound directly for Rome, or had they changes of passage to make en route? How long did they expect the voyage would take? Indicate upon the map and describe the voyage from Cæsarea to Fair Havens. What "Fast" is referred to in 27 : 9, and what time of the year is thereby indicated? Give a brief, accurate account of the tempest and shipwreck which befell the party after leaving Fair Havens, noting especially Paul's relations to the events. On what island were they stranded? Trace on the map the course, and describe the voyage, from Fair Havens to Malta. Consider the hand of God in this voyage of his apostle. Ascertain

something of the ofmethods and means navigation in Paul's time. Observe the graphic nature, completeness, and technical accuracy of the account of this voyage.

2. *The winter in Malta and journey to Rome.*—Locate upon the map and describe the island of Malta.   Describe the inhabitants of the island, as to their nationality, civilization, and language.   How wa the shipwrecked party received by them?   Consider the incident of the viper (28 : 3–6), Paul's escape, and the quaint superstition of the islanders regarding this.   Who was Publius, and what kindness did he extend to Paul and his companions?   What miracle did Paul perform at Publius' house, and why did he perform it?   Were other miraculous cures wrought at this time (28 : 9)?   How long was the stay in Malta, and when was the voyage to Rome resumed?   Indicate upon the map and describe the voyage from Malta to Puteoli.   From this point did they probably go by land to Rome?   Trace their course on this journey.   Who received Paul at Puteoli?   How came there to be Christians at that place?   Observe that the Christians are called "brethren" (28 : 14, 15).   Describe Paul's meeting with the Roman Christians who came out to welcome him on his approach to that city. Why was their greeting and interest of special importance and joy to Paul?   In what year, and at what season of the year, did Paul arrive in Rome?

3. *Paul and the Christians of Rome.*—Why does the New Testament contain no account of the establishment of Christianity in Rome? Is it evident from Rom. 1 : 13 ; 15 : 22–29 that Paul was not its founder? Is it probable also, from the following considerations, that Peter was not the founder either : the entire absence from Acts of any allusion to his presence in Rome ; the absence of any mention of his being, or having been there, from the epistles of Paul to the Romans and to the Philippians ; and the principle of Paul (Rom. 15 : 20) not to build on another man's foundation?   If not by Peter or Paul, or it would seem by any single individual of prominence, in what way, and when, was the gospel introduced into Rome?   Was it perhaps by Jews of Rome who were present in Jerusalem at the Pentecostal out-pouring and carried the gospel back with them (Acts 2 : 10) ; or by Hellenistic Jewish Christians who were dispersed from Jerusalem at Stephen's death (Acts 8 : 1 ; 11 : 19) ; or by Gentile Christians who had gone to Rome to live or to preach, from the several cities where Paul had established Christianity?   Is it probable, from Rom. 1 : 7 ; 16 : 5, that the Christians in Rome constituted several groups or churches

rather than a single organized body? Were there both Jews and
Gentiles in the Christian community or communities in Rome?
Consider the passages in the epistle to the Romans which indicate a
predominance of the Gentile element (Rom. 1:5, 6, 13–16; 6:19;
10:13, 14; 11:30, 31; 15:1, 8, 9, 15, 16). If mainly Gentile, would
the Roman Christians probably hold the Pauline views of Christianity,
and why? When, under what circumstances, and why, had Paul written
his epistle to the Romans? Why has the Acts said so little about the
Christians of Rome?

4. *Paul and the Jews of Rome.*— Did Paul, immediately upon his
arrival in Rome, set about to conciliate and convert the Jews of that
city? Describe his preliminary effort (28:17–22) to find out what
they had heard about him, and to remove all obstacles to his influence
and work among them. Consider in detail how his statement was
intended to effect this. Compare Paul's statement of his case with the
previous Acts account (chaps. 21–26) of the same. Consider carefully
the meaning of Acts 28:21, as to the surprising ignorance of the
Roman Jews concerning Paul's previous conflicts with the Jews everywhere else. How came the Roman Jews to know so very little (28:22)
about the gospel and the Christians when there were so many Christians, some of them converted Jews, in their own city? How large
was the attendance at Paul's second conference with the Jews of Rome?
Consider how Paul expounded to them at this time the relation of
Christianity to Judaism. What was the result of this presentation of
the gospel? Why did these Jews as a body reject Paul's teaching?
What warning did Paul give them before they went away? Consider
Paul's use of the Old Testament passage in 28:26, 27, and compare
other New Testament instances of its use (Matt. 13:14; Mark 4:12;
Luke 8:10; John 12:40; Rom. 11:8). Did Paul then turn with the
gospel, as on former occasions elsewhere, to the Gentiles of the city?
Observe and explain the omission from the Revised Version of Acts
28:29.

5. *Paul's Roman imprisonment and the Acts record.*— For how long
a time, and during what years, was Paul a prisoner at Rome? What
was the nature of his captivity (28:16, 30)? Was he allowed to carry
on his gospel ministry as he chose? In what way did he do so?
What two chief elements of his teaching are here (28:31) mentioned?
Study the epistles, as time permits, which Paul wrote during this period
(Colossians, Philemon, Ephesians, Philippians), for the light which
they throw upon his life and work at this time. Why does the Acts

narrative end so abruptly with 28:31 ? Did the trial and its conclusion come at the end of the two years' imprisonment ? Did the trial
result in condemnation or acquittal, was Paul put to death or released ?
If the latter, how long a time intervened before his death (in 64 A. D.
or later), and what was Paul doing during this period ? When and
why were Paul's epistles to Timothy and Titus written ? Consider
and explain the incompleteness of the Acts account of Paul's ministry
in Rome and the closing years of his career.

III. OBSERVATIONS AND TEACHINGS.

* For directions as to the work to be done under this head, see the statement at this point in Sec. 20.

Literature.—Upon this section see the commentaries on Acts, especially those
of GLOAG, HACKETT, MEYER, and the CAMBRIDGE BIBLE. Also McGIFFERT, History of Christianity in the Apostolic Age, pp. 356–439 ; WEIZSÄCKER, Apostolic Age
of the Christian Church, Vol. II, pp. 115–131; RAMSAY, St. Paul the Traveler, pp.
283–362; NEANDER, Planting and Training of the Christian Church, Vol. I, pp. 311–
318 ; FARRAR, Life and Work of St. Paul, chaps. 43 to 45 ; CONYBEARE AND HOWSON,
Life and Epistles of St. Paul, chaps. 23, 24 ; STIFLER, Introduction to the Book of
Acts, secs. xix, xx ; BIBLE DICTIONARY, articles Appii Forum, Aristarchus, Cauda
(Clauda), Euraquilo (Euroclydon), Fair Havens, Italy, Julius, Luke, Malta (Melita),
Paul, Phœnix (Phenice), Publius, Rome, Syracuse, Syrtis, Three Taverns.

REVIEW OF THE PRIMITIVE ERA OF CHRISTIANITY.

The Book of Acts.   30–63 A. D.   The Roman Empire.

I. THE ACTS RECORD.

1. Read through the entire book of Acts at one sitting (sixty to ninety minutes), endeavoring to bring the whole history to mind as one unit.

2. Observe the general portions of the book : chaps. 1–7, Christianity in Jerusalem ; chaps. 8–15, Christianity in Palestine and Syria ; chaps. 16–20, Christianity in Asia and Greece ; chaps. 21–28, Paul's Trials and Imprisonment.

3. Review carefully the outline of the history which is contained in the three main divisions, the sections and the paragraphs (for the divisions and sections see pages 3 and 4, for the paragraphs see under each ,section). This analysis should be studied until the divisions and sections, with the Acts passages, dates and localities can be written out from memory.

4. Note down the chief characteristics of the book of Acts as a history of the Apostolic Age, as to purpose, style, sources, material included, material excluded, proportionate length of the accounts of the several events, incidents and speeches, the naratives of miracles, the historical trustworthiness in general and in detail.

II. TIME AND ORDER OF EVENTS.

1. Review carefully the Chronological Chart of the Primitive Era of Christianity (page 2), observing whether, in view of your study, you would now change the date of, or rearrange, any of the events (consider the general note at the foot of the chart).

2. Commit to memory now, if you have not previously done so, this Chronological Chart, fixing in mind the time, the consecution, and the relative importance of the events.

III. GEOGRAPHY OF THE HISTORY.

1. Reconsider the fact, and its significance, that the Acts record is framed upon the geographical extension of Christianity.

2. State the five distinct steps of geographical progression of the

gospel as set forth in the Acts (see rule column on the extreme left of the Chronological Chart), giving the dates over which each step extends, and a brief description of the circumstances.

3. Sketch a map of the Roman Empire about the Mediterranean Sea, on which pictorially represent the spread of Christianity by five concentric circles about Jerusalem, and mark upon the circumference of each circle the date when the gospel reached this district, and the Acts passage which records the fact.

IV. ORGANIZATION OF THE CHRISTIANS.

1. The organization of the church was a natural and gradual growth from an almost unorganized condition to a somewhat complex form of government adapted to the organic life and work of the church. Each element of the organization therefore needs to be considered, first, in its individual aspects, second, in its relational aspects. Consider (1) when each element was introduced into the organization, (2) why it was introduced, (3) what its relation was to the organization into which it came, (4) what its subsequent individual and relational development was.

2. The most important topics which call for this treatment are the following:

    (1) the original apostles.   (4) Deacons.
    (2) other church leaders   (5) Prophets.
        called apostles.   (6) Evangelists.
    (3) Elders (presbyters,   (7) Pastors.
        bishops).   (8) Teachers.

    (9) the difference between orders and functions with reference to the foregoing church officers.

    (10) absence of any general, comprehensive church officers other than the apostles.

    (11) the unity of the local church.

    (12) the independence of the local church.

    (13) the method of conducting business in church meetings.

    (14) the various elements of which the churches were composed.

    (15) the method of church discipline.

    (16) the conditions of church membership.

    (17) variations in the form of church organization in different localities.

V. Environment of the Christians.

1. The environment in which the Christians found themselves constantly underwent modification and change, both by reason of territorial expansion and through the acquisition of adherents to the cause. The environment, therefore, should be viewed separately in each of the three main divisions of the Acts history.

2. The general topics for consideration in each period will be:
    (1) the particular parts of the world in which Christianity had become established.
    (2) the chief centers of Christian influence.
    (3) the relation to the church of the civil power—the Roman government.
    (4) the relation to the church of the Jewish people in general.
    (5) the relation to the church of the Gentile people in general.
    (6) the relation between Jewish and Gentile Christians.
    (7) the conflict between Christianity and Judaism.
    (8) the conflict between Christianity and Heathenism.

VI. Institutions of the Christians.

Reconsider fully the institutions of the Christian church, each in turn, as regards its origin, significance, manner of observation, modification during the era (if any), and influence. The most important institutions of the church were the following:

    (1) baptism.   (8) private religious services.
    (2) the Lord's Supper.   (9) places of worship.
    (3) the agape.   (10) preaching.
    (4) Sunday.   (11) instruction.
    (5) other sacred days.   (12) sacred music and hymns.
    (6) creeds.   (13) prayer.
    (7) public services.   (14) charitable contributions.

VII. Belief and Teaching of the Christians.

Review carefully the belief and teaching of the primitive Christians, both as respects theology and as respects ethics, as they are recorded in the book of Acts.

1. The theological belief and teaching of the primitive Christians appears mainly in the sermons and speeches of the Acts: by Peter in chapters 2, 3, 4, 5, 10, 11, 15; by Stephen in chapter

10 ; by James in chapter 15 ; and by Paul in chapters 13, 14, 17, 20, 22, 24, 26, 28.   This belief and teaching may be reconsidered under the following topics :

(1) God.	(8) redemption.
(2) Christ.	(9) the Christian life.
(3) the Holy Spirit.	(10) the second advent of Christ.
(4) the spiritual nature of man.	(11) the resurrection.
	(12) the judgment.
(5) sin.	(13) the consummation of the kingdom.
(6) the Mosaic law.	
(7) justification by faith.	(14) Old Testament Scriptures.

2. The ethical belief and teaching may be reconsidered under the following topics :

    (1) individual morals.
    (2) duties to existing government.
    (3) duties toward social institutions, e. g., slavery.
    (4) duties of family life.
    (5) duties toward the weaker brethren.
    (6) Christian virtues.
    (7) Christian graces.

VIII. DAILY LIFE OF THE CHRISTIANS.

Reconsider the characteristics of the life which the Christians lived, both individually and as members of the Christian community. Observe also whether there were material differences in the daily life of the Christians between one and another of the three main divisions of the Acts history.   The review may be made on the basis of the following topics :

(1) fellowship.	(10) social life.
(2) unity.	(11) division of duties.
(3) charity.	(12) manners of employment.
(4) coöperation.	(13) growth in numbers.
(5) property relations.	(14) growth in grace.
(6) loyalty to the gospel.	(15) miracle-working.
(7) fervency and worshipfulness.	(16) prophesying.
	(17) speaking with tongues.
(8) zeal and activity for the cause.	(18) interpretation of tongue speaking.
(9) individual morals.	

IX. The Leading Gospel Workers.

Review the Christian leaders of the primitive era, observing the particular division or divisions of the history within which the career of each one fell. Consider them respectively as regards their personal characteristics, their official characteristics, their special missions, their influence upon Christianity. The following workers at least should be so considered, and others may be added as seems fitting :

(1) Peter.	(7) Barnabas.
(2) James.	(8) Mark.
(3) John.	(9) Silas.
(4) Stephen.	(10) Timothy.
(5) Philip.	(11) Titus.
(6) Paul.	(12) Luke.

X. Divine Guidance and Instruction.

1. Reconsider the continual and loving presence of Christ with his followers, the constant evidence of God's hand in the events and the experiences of the primitive era of Christianity. Review the providential aspects of the life of Peter, and of the life of Paul; similarly of other prominent Christian workers. Consider the Providence which guided the spread of the gospel throughout the pagan world. May it be said that the career of Christianity, from first to last of the Apostolic Age, through every moment of its existence, was sustained, directed and developed by the divine wisdom, love and power?

2. Reconsider, as fully as time permits, the many lessons for present day Christian life, internal and external, individual and collective, which God has given to us in the events and experiences of the Apostolic Age.

www.ingramcontent.com/pod-product-compliance
Lightning Source LLC
Chambersburg PA
CBHW032015010726
47493CB00007B/2416